INTRODUCTION TO CONTRACT LAW

REVISION GUIDE

Law Series: 3

INTRODUCTION TO CONTRACT LAW

REVISION GUIDE

Dr Johanna Hoekstra

First published in 2021 by TRANSNATIONAL PRESS LONDON in the United Kingdom, 13 Stamford Place, Sale, M33 3BT, UK.

www.tplondon.com

Paperback

ISBN: 978-1-912997-74-9

Digital

ISBN: 978-1-80135-080-8

Cover Design: Nihal Yazgan

Transnational Press London Ltd. is a company registered in England and Wales No. 8771684.

INTRODUCTION TO CONTRACT LAW

REVISION GUIDE

Dr Johanna Hoekstra

TRANSNATIONAL PRESS LONDON

2021

CONTENTS

ABBREVIATIONS

B2B: Business to Business

B2C: Business to Consumer

B2G: Business to Government

C2C: Consumer to Consumer

CISG: Convention for Contracts for the International Sale of Goods 1980

CMA: Competition and Market Authority

CRA: Consumer Rights Act 2015

EC: European Community

ECJ: European Court of Justice

EU: European Union

HMRC: Her Majesty's Revenue and Customs

LLP: Limited Liability Partnerships

LTD: Limited

SME: Small and Medium Enterprises

SOGA: Sale of Goods Act 1979

UCTA: Unfair Contract Terms Act 1977

UK: United Kingdom

UN: United Nations

UTCCR: Unfair Terms in Consumer Contracts Regulations

ABOUT THE AUTHOR

Dr Johanna Hoekstra is a lecturer at the School of Law & Centre for Human Rights at the University of Essex. Prior to this she worked as a lecturer at the University of Greenwich. Johanna has a PhD in international commercial law from the University of Essex and master's degrees from Birkbeck College and the University of Bordeaux.

FOREWORD

This book discusses the principles and rules of general contract law in England & Wales. It examines the key points and rules of contract law, starting with the formation of the contract and ending with the remedies for breach of contract. In this it follows the structure most used in contract law modules at universities. Please also note that this book takes into account developments of the law up until July 2021.

Contracts are at the foundation of life in society. To live in society, it is not possible to avoid concluding a variety of contracts on a mostly daily basis. All of us are part of a myriad of contracts. We need contracts to have food, to clothe ourselves, to have a place to live, to travel, to work, to study, to keep in touch with friends and family that are far away, and for countless other reasons. The legal framework for contracts is therefore of both practical and academic importance. Contract law helps you to understand when an agreement becomes an enforceable contract, what elements are necessary for a contract to be valid, under which circumstances a contract is not valid, and what happens when a contract is breached.

Contract law is a core module in legal higher education in the UK. Contract law is also an important basis for many other law modules including maritime law, company law, commercial law, and arbitration law. This book gives a clear oversight of the main issues of key contract law topics. It summarises the issues in a concise and precise manner and uses practical examples throughout to clarify how the law is applied. Key cases are used to explain and illustrate the principles of the law. This book is an ideal companion guide for exam revisions. The chapters follow a question-and-answer model that makes it easy to find information on a specific issue. The chapters end with a problem-solving scenario on key issues of the topic and a list with key cases which will be helpful in preparing for examinations. At the end of the book, you find a further reading list and a set of sample multiple-choice questions which can be used to help prepare for the first stage of the SQE examination that will be introduced in September 2021.

I would like to thank Transnational Press London, Dr Özgür Heval Çınar, Ms Hülya Ak, the colleagues that I worked with teaching contract law, and my family.

Dr Johanna Hoekstra

CHAPTER I

INTRODUCTION

Learning Outcomes:

After reading this chapter, you should be able to understand:

- ✓ What a contract is;
- ✓ The different types of contract;
- ✓ The sources of contract law;
- ✓ Why we need contract law.

Questions and Answers:

1. What is a contract?

A contract is a legally binding agreement between two or more parties that creates rights and obligations for these parties. English contract law has no formal definition of a contract.

A classic definition is given by Treitel in the *Law of Contract* (Editor: E Peel, 15th edition, Sweet & Maxwell): *"An agreement giving rise to obligations which are enforced or recognised by law. The factor which distinguishes contractual from other legal obligations is that they are based on the agreement of the contracting parties."*

Contracts can be concluded in writing, orally, or through conduct (***simple contracts***). Only in exceptional cases the contract needs to be in writing. These are ***contracts by deeds***. Examples are contracts containing a guarantee, contracts related to the sale, transfer, option, or lease of land and property (Law of Property (Miscellaneous Provisions) Act 1989).

The parties must enter into the agreement freely. The object of the contract should not be illegal.

For there to be a valid contract there should be:

Offer and acceptance ***(See Chapter II)***

Intention to create legal relations ***(See Chapter III)***

Certainty of agreement ***(See Chapter III)***

Consideration ***(See Chapter IV)***

The parties should have the ***capacity*** to enter into a contract ***(See Chapter VI)***

Vitiating factors in the formation of the contract can make the contract void or voidable. These factors include:

Misrepresentation ***(See Chapter IX)***

Duress and undue influence ***(See Chapter X)***

Mistake ***(See Chapter XI)***

The parties decide on their rights and obligations in ***the terms of the contract (See Chapter VII)*** although the law can limit the use of certain terms such as ***exclusion clauses (See Chapter VIII)***.

If a party ***breaches the contract***, the other party is entitled to certain ***remedies*** including damages ***(See Chapter XIII)*** unless the party breaching the contract has a lawful excuse such as ***frustration*** of contract ***(See Chapter XII)***. The contract can only create obligations between the parties and cannot create any obligations for ***third parties***, although in some cases the contract can create certain rights for third parties ***(See Chapter V)***.

2. What is the difference between a unilateral contract and a bilateral contract?

A unilateral contract is a one-way exchange: The offeror makes a promise that he will do X in exchange for Y and the offeree can accept that promise through the performance of Y.

Examples are promises of rewards in exchange for finding an object or for testing a product.

Example: John has lost his dog. He puts a notice on a streetlamp which states that he will give a £1,000 for the safe return of his dog. Mary finds John's dog and brings the dog back to him. By bringing the dog back to John she has accepted the offer and John is now contractually obliged to give Mary £1,000.

A bilateral contract is a two-way exchange. The offeror offers to do X in exchange for Y and the offeree accepts this by stating to the offeree that he will do Y in exchange for X. The vast majority of contracts are bilateral contracts. Examples are sales contracts, employment contracts, or hire-purchase agreements.

Example: John asks Mary if she wants to buy his bike for £100. Mary accepts to buy the bike for a £100. John gives the bike to Mary and Mary gives £100 to John.

3. What categories of contract are there?

Contracts can be divided in several categories.

Firstly, we can divide categories in domestic and international contracts.

Domestic contracts: The contracting parties all have their place of business/residence in the same country and there are no other international elements to the contract.

International contracts: The contract contains an international element that is relevant to the contract. Internationality is often measured through the parties having their place of business/habitual residence in different countries, but sometimes a wider scope is necessary to understand whether the contract is international.

Secondly, contracts can be divided by ***the capacity in which the parties act***:

- Business to Business (B2B) – a commercial contract
- Business to Consumer (B2C) – a consumer contract
- Consumer to Consumer (C2C)
- Business to Government (B2G)

Specific legislation often applies to consumer contracts. This has the aim to offer more protection to the consumer.

Thirdly, contracts can be divided by ***the type of transaction***. This would include for example:

- Sale
- Franchise
- Leasing
- Insurance
- Carriage of goods
- Services
- Distribution
- Employment
- Tenancy
- Financing…

This book is about ***the general principles and rules of English contract law***. These are applicable to contracts in general. This is what is taught on core undergraduate contract law modules at universities in England & Wales. For specific type contracts there is often specialised legislation. These types of contracts are studied in more advanced modules of commercial and contract law or on modules on specific areas such as employment law, carriage of goods law, and company law.

4. What are the sources of contract law?

Contract law is mainly common law. That is to say that it is based on the precedents established by case law. Contract law is private law. It is part of ***the law of obligations***, alongside tort law and the law of unjust enrichment. There are some key statutory instruments in contract law:

- ✓ Misrepresentation Act 1967
- ✓ Trade Description Act 1968
- ✓ Unfair Contract Terms Act 1977
- ✓ Sales of Goods Act 1979
- ✓ Consumer Rights Act 2015

Other statutory legislation exists for specific type contracts.

Consumer contract law in the United Kingdom (UK) is heavily shaped by European Union (EU) law. Following the UK leaving the EU (Brexit) this legislation has been incorporated into domestic law, although the UK could decide to make changes to the legislation in the future.

Principles arising out of ***equity*** are also a source of contract law. These include for instance undue influence, promissory estoppel, and specific performance.

Transnational commercial non-state rules play a key role in shaping practices and principles of international contract law. These include notably:

- The UNIDROIT Principles of International Commercial Contracts
- The Principles of European Contract Law
- The Draft Common Frame of Reference
- The INCOTERMS

The international merchant community created and shaped their own rules, principles, and obligations through the ***lex mercatoria*** which continues to play a key role in transnational commerce.

Usages and custom are important in contract law. Trade usages are treated as implied terms of the contract. Contracts are interpreted through usage and custom where appropriate.

Finally, it should be noted that it is often said that the first source of contract law is ***the contract*** itself. This is because when deciding a dispute between the contracting parties, the court will first look at the contract itself to decide what the parties have agreed on their rights and obligations. The contract creates legally enforceable rights between the parties. The court will as much as possible give effect to what the parties have agreed.

5. Is the law different for international contracts?

In the UK no specific legislation exists for most international contracts. If English law is the applicable law, the same rules and principles apply as for domestic contracts, although the court might take the internationality of the contract into account in its interpretation. For some specific type contracts there is separate legislation. For instance:

- *Carriage of goods by sea contracts* (The Hague-Visby Rules)
- *Carriage of goods by rail contracts* (Uniform Rules concerning the Contract of International Carriage of Goods by Rail (CIM))
- *International interests in aircraft equipment* (Protocol to the Convention on International Interests in Mobile Equipment on Matters Specific to Aircraft Equipment (Cape Town Convention).
- *Carriage of goods by air contracts* (Montreal Convention for the Unification of Certain Rules for International Carriage by Air)

For ***international sale contracts*** the UK has adopted the Uniform Laws on International Sales Act 1967 (based on the United Nations Conventions for a Uniform Law on the International Sale of Goods and a Uniform Law on the Formation of Contracts for the International Sale of Goods). This is an opt in law: That is to say this law is only applicable if the parties have specified in their contract that it should be regulated by the Act.

More than 2/3 of international sales worldwide are covered by the Convention for Contracts for the International Sale of Goods 1980 (CISG). This convention is ratified by 94 countries worldwide. The UK has not ratified the CISG and therefore it is not applicable in contracts where the governing law is English law.

6. Why do we need a contract law?

The parties to the contract can decide on the terms of the contract and regulate all aspects of their transaction.

However, what if:

- One of the parties does not adhere to what was agreed?
- The parties did not foresee an eventuality that arises?
- Only minimal provisions are laid out in the contract?
- One of the parties was not being truthful or put pressure on another party?

- A mistake was made?
- The object of the contract was illegal?
- The circumstances have changed, and the contract can no longer be performed?

Contract law is needed to solve these issues. It defines when an agreement is enforceable. It resolves disputes between the parties if they are in disagreement over what they have agreed. It provides certainty and predictability for the contracting parties.

The role of the court is to give effect to the intentions of the parties, to enforce obligations that the parties have agreed on, to interpret the contract when the parties do not agree on this, to ensure that the contract does not run contrary to public policy, to provide a level of protection to the parties, and to decide on remedies in case of breach of contract. The court does not write the agreement for the parties, it merely gives effect to what the parties have agreed.

7. What are presumptions?

To facilitate contracting, ***the law assumes in certain situations X is true***. It is then up to the party claiming that X is not true in their specific case to present enough evidence to the court that ***rebuts the presumption***. If the presumption is rebutted, the court will no longer hold that X is true in this particular case.

8. What are vitiating factors?

Contracts are the expression of the free will of the parties. Vitiating factors disturb the free will of the parties. A vitiating factor can make the contract voidable or void.

These include:

- Misrepresentation
- Mistake
- Duress
- Undue influence

9. What do we mean with objective v subjective?

Often, to decide how the contract should be interpreted the court will look at the objective intention of the parties. It applies the *reasonable person test*: based on the available evidence, how would a reasonable person interpret the contract?

Using a subjective interpretation would cause problems because it is impossible to know the state of the mind of a person. Lord Denning in ***Storer v Manchester City Council [1974]***: *"In contracts you do not look into the actual intent in a man's mind. You look at what he said and did. A contract is formed when there is, to all outward appearances, a contract. A man cannot get out of a contract by saying, 'I did not intent to contract', if by his word he has done so."*

10. What is meant by freedom of contract?

Freedom of contract means that the parties voluntarily enter into the agreement.

Freedom TO Contract – parties can enter into a contract with whom they want

Freedom OF Contract – parties can decide on the terms and conditions in their contract

Freedom FROM Contract – parties can decide not to enter into a contract.

Freedom of contract was the key legal principle of English contract law in the 19th century, but this has gradually changed: principles such as fairness and reasonableness have contributed to creating a stronger legal framework that offers more protection to the parties.

The law intervenes in the freedom of contract to re-address unequal bargaining power, protect the weaker party, and address public policy concerns. The law must find a balance between freedom and protection. Professors Brownsword and Adams have written a key treatise on these two key approaches to contract law: 'market-individualism' (promoting freedom) and 'consumer-welfarism (promoting protection).[1] Freedom of contract promotes certainty and stability as the parties can be sure that their agreement will be honoured. Protection creates a more level playing field for weaker parties and encourages fairness and justice.

---

[1] John N Adams & Roger Brownsword, *'The ideologies of contract'* (1987) Legal Studies 205.

CHAPTER II

OFFER AND ACCEPTANCE

Learning Outcomes:

After reading this chapter, you should be able to understand:

- ✓ What an offer is;
- ✓ The difference between an offer, a request for information, and an invitation to treat;
- ✓ How an offer can be accepted;
- ✓ The difference between acceptance, a counteroffer, and a request for information.

Questions and Answers:

1.What is an offer?

An offer is a definite statement that shows a willingness by the person making it to be bound by the terms of that statement. It can be made orally, through conduct, or in writing.

The person who makes the offer is called the ***offeror*** and the person to whom the offer is made is called the ***offeree***. An offer can be made to a particular person, to a group of people, or to the world at large. The offer is the first port of call in the search to find out whether there is a contract between the parties.

Whether a person intended to make an offer should be ascertained ***objectively***, based on the intentions of the offeror as understood by a reasonable person (***Moran v Salford University [1993]***). The court examines the communications between the parties to discern whether objectively there is an intention to be bound by the offer (***Storer v Manchester* CC *[1974]***).

Courts will ***not enforce offers that are too vague***. For example, an actress was offered a role in a play in exchange for a 'west-end rate' salary. When the role was retracted, and the actress sued, the court stated that the term 'west end rate' was too vague and uncertain, which meant there was no offer (***Loftus v Roberts [1902]***).

Railway and bus timetables are considered offers which can be accepted by passengers who buy railway tickets or board buses (***Denton v Great Northern Railway Vo. [1856]***). The Transport Act 1962 and the Railways Act 1993 prevent contractual liability if the transportation company does not adhere to the timetable.

An automatic vending machine is an offer that is accepted when it is prompted to issue a ticket or the product (***Thorton v Shoe Lane Parking [1971]***).

The offer should be distinguished from other statements made during the negotiations such as ***representations, enquiries, mere puffs, and invitations to treat.***

A request for information is not an offer (***Harvey v Facey [1893]***). A telegraph was sent to the defendant asking what the lowest price was they would sell a specific property for. The defendant replied: 'lowest cash price £900.' The plaintiffs responded, 'we agree to buy for the £900 asked by you.' The defendant did not reply to this message. The plaintiffs alleged that a contract had been formed as they had accepted the offer made by the defendant. The court held that the first telegraph had been an enquiry and that the response of the defendant was not an offer, but a response to that enquiry. The final telegraph sent by the plaintiff constituted an offer which the defendant did not accept. Therefore, there was no contract.

2. What is an invitation to treat?

An invitation to treat occurs when ***one party invites the other party to make an offer.*** It is a statement made as part of the negotiations. To distinguish an offer from an invitation to treat the court looks at the objective intent of the parties by taking into account the circumstances, examining the communications between the parties, and establishing any trade usages and course of dealing between the parties.

The court also uses certain **presumptions** to distinguish between an offer and an invitation to treat; these presumptions are rebuttable. The court presumes a certain scenario is true, but if there is any evidence to the contrary the court will take this evidence into account.

There is a presumption that the following are invitations to treat:

Display of goods in a shop are considered an invitation to treat. The customer makes the offer by presenting the item to the cashier. The cashier then accepts the offer (***Pharmaceutical Society of Great Britain v Boots Cash Chemists [1953]*** and ***Fisher v Bell [1961]***).

The same rules apply grosso modo to sales through websites (Electronic Commerce (EC Directive) Regulations 2002).

Advertisements are considered invitations to treat (***Partridge v Crittenden [1968]***) because if the advertisement was an offer the seller would need to have an unlimited stock of what is being advertisement as they could not know in advance how many people would accept the offer (***Grainger & Son v Gough [1986]***). If a person responds indicating his willingness to buy what is advertised, then this is considered the offer which the advertiser can then accept. The advertiser is not compelled to accept and can refuse the offer.

This presumption is rebuttable if the advertisement contains such precise instructions that it leaves nothing to be decided. ***Lefkowitz v. Great Minneapolis Surplus Store [1957]*** is an American contract law case where the defendant posted an advertisement stating: *Saturday 9 A.M. Sharp 3 Brand New Fur Coats Worth to $100.00. First Come First Served $1 Each.*

Mr Lefkowitz was the first customer in the store on Saturday. The owner refused to sell to him arguing that the products were intended only for women. Mr Lefkowitz went to court because the ad did not say anything about only women being allowed to buy the clothes. The defendant argued that the ad was an invitation to treat and that therefore he was not compelled to sell to Mr Lefkowitz. The court held that the advertisement was precise enough to constitute an offer as it was '*clear, definite, and explicit, and leaves nothing open for negotiation.*'

Another example is the famous case of ***Carlill v Carbolic Smoke Ball Company [1983]*** which is also the key case on ***unilateral offers***. The Carbolic Smoke Ball Company placed a newspaper advertisement which promoted the use of a product called a carbolic smoke ball which they claimed could stay off the flu. The advertisement stated that any person who uses the ball three times a day for two weeks and who would contract *'influenza, cold, or any disease caused by taking cold'* was entitled to a £100 reward. Mrs Carlill used the product as indicated but she did get influenza and therefore asked for the £100. The defendant suggested that the advertisement was too vague to be an offer, that it was meant to be mere sales talk, and that a contract cannot be made to the whole world.

The court stated that it is possible to make an offer to the world at large (this is a unilateral offer), that the advertisement was precise enough to be an offer, and that by depositing a £1,000 into an account for this purpose, the company had shown it was serious about the offer. Mrs Carlill accepted the offer, not when she bought the smoke ball, but when she completed the treatment as prescribed in the advertisement.

For ***auctions,*** the auctioneer makes an invitation to treat, and the ensuing bid is considered the offer which the auctioneer can accept by the fall of the hammer (***Payne v Cave [1789]***) (codified in the Sale of Goods Act 1979, Section 57(2) (SOGA).

A distinction is made between an auction with or without a reserve price (***Barry v Davies [2000]***). If the auction is without reserve price, then the auctioneer should sell to the person who made the highest bona fide bid.

The request for a ***tender*** (circular) is considered an invitation to treat and the tender itself constitutes the offer (***Spencer v Harding [1870]***). A tender does give rise to certain obligations: When the tender is submitted in compliance with the rules it should be considered along with the other tenders that were submitted in compliance (***Blackpool and Fylde Areo Club Ltd v Blackpool Borough Council [1990]***).

3.When is the offer terminated?

An offer may lapse on:

- The expiry of the stipulated period for which the offer is open;
- The expiry of any conditions (express or implied);
- The passage of a reasonable period of time.

What a reasonable period of time is depends on the subject matter of the contract (***Ramsgate Victoria Hotel v Montefiore [1866]***). For instance, if the subject matter is a good/service where the market is volatile (such as charter parties and shares), or the goods are perishable (such as fruit and vegetables) the reasonable period would be shorter than for goods/services in a more stable market (such as antiques and machinery) or which do not perish/change as fast (such as land and building materials).

The offer can be ***revoked*** at any time before acceptance is communicated (***Routledge v Grant [1828]***). This is even the case if a specific date which lies in the future was communicated to the offeree – the offeror does not have to wait for that day to revoke the offer.

Exception: If the offer is contained in a deed or the offeree has given consideration to the offeror then the offer cannot be revoked before the expiry date.

A unilateral offer cannot be revoked once performance has started, but the promise does not have to be honoured until performance is completed.

The revocation only becomes effective if it is communicated to the offeree before acceptance takes effect

A postal revocation is not effective on posting, but only when it is brought to the mind of the offeree (***Henthorn v Fraser [1892]***) or when it would be reasonable to expect the offeree to get notice of the revocation (for instance when it arrives during office hours at a business premise). The same is true for ***other ways to communicate the revocation***: It is only effective when received. If the revocation is made to a business, there is no requirement that this is read by a specific person in that business (***The Brimnes [1975]***).

An advertisement can be revoked by placing a similar advertisement (for instance, in the same newspaper).

The offer can also be revoked by ***a reliable third party*** acting without the offeror's authority (***Dickinson v Dodds [1876]***). The offeror must show that under the circumstances it would have been reasonable for the offeree to assume that this information was accurate.

4. What is acceptance?

Acceptance is a statement (written, oral, or through conduct) that shows a willingness to be bound by the terms of an offer. ***Acceptance must be unequivocal, unqualified, and communicated.***

A different communication method from how the offer was communicated can be used to communicate acceptance provided that ***it is not less advantageous to the offeror than the method through which the offer was made***. If the offer prescribes the manner in which acceptance should be communicated, then ***acceptance is only valid if it is communicated in the way prescribed in the offer***.

Silence cannot constitute acceptance (***Felthouse v Bindley [1862]***).

Acceptance must be made in response to an offer (***Fitch v Snedaker [1868]***).

Example: If Mike sends an email to Aziza asking if he can buy her computer for a £100 and at the same time Aziza sends a text to Mike asking if he is willing to buy her computer for £100, there are two offers, but no acceptance even though the parties want the same thing (***Tinn v Hoffman [1873]***). Therefore, there is no valid contract between Aziza and Mike until one of the two responds directly to the offer of the other.

Sam loses his dog and puts up a poster offering £1,000 to the person that finds the dog. Sam's neighbour Astrid sees Sam's dog in the street and brings the dog back to Sam. Astrid was not aware of the reward and was just rendering neighbourly service. Should Sam now still pay Astrid?

An offer can only be accepted if ***the offeree is aware of the offer***. Therefore, the answer is no. At the same time, the motive of the person carrying out the act is not important (***Williams v Carwardine [1833]***) and the burden to prove Astrid was not aware of the offer is on Sam.

5. What is the battle of the forms?

Businesses frequently use ***standard terms and conditions*** in their contract. If the contract is with a consumer this is not an issue because the consumer will not have their own standard terms. However, if the contract is between two businesses, then both will want to use their own standard terms. The offeror will usually send their standard terms and conditions along with the offer. The offeree will send their standard terms and conditions along with acceptance. This might then be followed by the offeror sending his own terms along with the acknowledgment of receipt, and so forth. This is called the battle of the forms.

The general rule is that the party which last sent its terms and conditions without getting a reply prevails and thus ***the last shot usually wins*** (***Butler Machine Tool Co Ltd v Ex-cell-O Corporation Ltd [1979]***). It can be difficult to ascertain which party's standard terms and conditions prevail if there have been multiple (sometimes simultaneous) communications between the parties.

If acceptance must completely match the offer, there would be no acceptance if the terms and conditions sent by the offeree do not match those of the offeror. However, as standard terms and conditions seldom go to the core of the offer, a degree of inconsistency between offer and acceptance is acceptable, as long as it is not on material points (***Matthieson Gee (Ayshire) Ltd v Quigley [1952]***).

There are two stages in the battle of the forms:

1. Have the parties reached agreement?
2. On what terms and conditions have they reached agreement?

6. What is a counteroffer?

An acceptance that materially alters the conditions of the contract is considered as a counteroffer. ***The counteroffer destroys the offer (Hyde v Wrench [1840])***.

Example: Rasheed offers to sell his bike to Tom for £150. Tom says he would like to buy the bike for a £100. Rasheed refuses. Tom replies that he is ok with paying the £150. Rasheed says that he no longer wants to sell the bike to Tom.

Rasheed has made an offer. Tom did not accept the offer but made a counteroffer. Rasheed did not accept the counteroffer. Tom now wants to accept the original offer, but he can no longer do so because by making a counteroffer Tom has destroyed the original offer. Rasheed's offer is no longer valid. Therefore, Rasheed does not have to sell the bike to Tom.

A counteroffer should be distinguished from a request for ***further information***. In ***Stevenson v Mclean [1880]*** Mclean offered to sell iron at 40s per ton. Stevenson asked Mclean whether he would 'accept 40 for delivery over 2 months or the longest time you would give.' Stevenson then sent a telegram accepting the offer, but Mclean sold the iron to another party, arguing that Stevenson's initial response was a counteroffer. The court held that Stevenson's response was a request for information which did not destroy the offer and his acceptance was therefore valid.

7. When is acceptance communicated?

Acceptance takes place on ***receipt***. In ***Entores Ltd v Miles Far East Corp [1955]*** the claimants made an offer by telex to the defendants, a company based in Amsterdam. The defendants accepted the offer by telex. A conflict arose between the contracting parties and a key question was where the contract was concluded. Was this in Amsterdam where the telex was sent or in London where the telex was received? The court held that the contract was formed when acceptance was received in London.

The general rule is thus that ***acceptance is valid upon receipt.***

When the contracting parties are in direct contact (because they are together in the same room or speaking on the telephone), it is easy to determine that acceptance was received. However, if acceptance takes place by email, fax, or through text message it is not always easy to know whether the other party received the acceptance. What happens when there is a technological issue on the side of the offeror of which the offeree is not aware? For instance, the offeree communicates acceptance through email, the computer of the offeror is not working, and the offeror has thus not seen his emails. The offeree would not be aware that his acceptance was not received.

Another issue could be that the offeree communicates his acceptance by sending an email on Saturday evening which is not read until Monday. Should the offeree know that his acceptance has not been received until Monday? And what happens if the offeror claims that he has not seen the acceptance of his offer, even during working hours?

In those type of situations, it is assumed that ***acceptance takes effect during normal business hours*** (***Mondial Shipping and Chartering v Asarte Shipping Ltd [1995]***) and that ***technological issues of which the offeree could not be aware do not affect acceptance.*** Acceptance does not have to be read by a particular person; it is sufficient that it has been received by the business (***The Brimnes [1975]***).

There is one important exception on the rule that acceptance is valid upon receipt. This is called the ***postal rule***. It means that the acceptance of an offer through the post is ***valid when posted and not when received*** (***Adams v Lindsell [1818]***).

There are some limitations on the postal rule:

1. The letter of acceptance must be properly addressed.
2. The letter must be properly posted (***Re Household Fire Insurance v Grant [1879]***).
3. If the offeror has stated that the offer cannot be accepted by post the postal rule does not apply.
4. The postal rule only applies 'where the circumstances are such that it must have been within the contemplation of the parties that, according to the ordinary usages of mankind, the post might be used as a means of communicating the acceptance of an offer' (***Henthorn v Fraser [1892]***).

The postal rule does not apply to telexes, emails, and other forms of electronic communication (***Brinkibon Ltd v Stahag Stahl [1983]*** and ***Thomas v BPE Solicitors (A Firm) [2010]***). The postal rule only applies to acceptance, it does not apply to making an offer or revoking an offer; in those cases, the offer or revocation by post are valid upon receipt of the letter (***Byrne & Co v Leon Van Tien Hoven & Co [1880]***).

Summary:

- An offer is an expression of a willingness to create a binding agreement.
- An offer must be definite, invite acceptance, and be communicated to the offeree.
- An offer must be distinguished from an invitation to treat and a request for information.
- The offer can be revoked at any time before it is accepted (unless consideration was provided, or it is contained in a deed).

- Goods displayed in shops, advertisements, auctions, and tenders are presumed to be invitations to treat but these presumptions are rebuttable.
- If no specific form is prescribed, acceptance can be through any means of communication provided the method is not less advantageous than the method through which the offer was communicated.
- Acceptance takes place on receipt; the postal rule is the exception and acceptance by post takes place on despatch (provided this would have been within the contemplation of the parties).
- Silence does not constitute acceptance.

Problem Question:

Luke wants to sell his bike. On 5 December, he places an advertisement in the local newspaper: 'For sale: mountain bike, 20 gears, green frame, in prime condition £400.' He gives his mobile, number, email and house address.

Luke receives an email from Aurora. Aurora asks whether Luke would be willing to sell the bike for £300. Aurora then phones her friend Ethan who has told her that he is looking for a mountain bike and asks him what price he would be willing to pay for such a bike. Ethan says he would be willing to pay £450. Aurora asks whether that is as high as he will go and whether he would consider perhaps paying £500. Ethan says he will think about it and get back to her.

Aurora receives an email from Luke who says that he will not accept £300 for the bike but that he can sell it for £350 if she is interested. Aurora tries to contact Ethan, but he is not answering his phone. She sends him a text message saying that she will take the £450 for the mountain bike. Later that day Aurora wants to message Luke to say that she will pay the £350 for the mountain bike. She realises her internet is not working and therefore she sends a letter by post to Luke.

The following day, Ethan sees Luke's advertisement in the newspaper. Ethan calls Luke and asks him whether he is willing to sell the bike to him for £400. Luke agrees and says he will sell for that price. After Ethan hangs up, he sees Aurora's message. When the post arrives Luke also sees Aurora's letter.

Is there a valid contract here?

Luke's newspaper advertisement can be considered an invitation to treat as this is the general presumption for an advertisement (***Partridge v Crittenden [1968]***) and his ad is not specific enough that it can be considered an offer. Therefore, when Aurora sends him the email in response to the ad, she is making an offer. In his response Luke does not accept the offer because he does not agree with the price she proposes. Instead, he makes a counteroffer which destroys Aurora's offer (***Hyde v Wrench [1840]***). When Aurora responds by sending a letter, she accepts Luke's offer. The postal rule states that acceptance is effective upon posting and not upon receipt ***(Adams v Lindsell [1818]***). However, the postal rule would only apply if a communication by post was within the contemplation of the parties (***Henthorn v Fraser [1892]***). Would this be the case here? Luke put his house address in the ad so he could have expected some communication by post. However, the communication between Luke and Aurora took place by email and the offer Luke made to Aurora was by email. The general rule is that acceptance should come by means that are not less advantageous than the offer. Therefore, the postal rule might not apply.

Aurora did not initially make an offer to Ethan, but she made a request for information as she asked him how much he was willing to pay (***Harvey v Facey [1893]***). Ethan responded to that request for information. There was no clear offer yet. When Aurora texted Ethan telling him, she was willing to sell for £450 she made an offer to Ethan. Ethan never responded and therefore never accepted the offer as an offer cannot be accepted through silence (***Felthouse v Bindley [1862]***).

Luke and Ethan made an agreement over the telephone whereby Ethan made an offer that Luke accepted.

Luke and Ethan have a contract.

Ethan and Aurora do not have a contract.

Luke and Aurora might have a contract. Luke made a clear offer to Aurora. The question is whether the manner in which she accepted the offer is valid. If the postal rule applies, then Aurora has accepted the offer and a contract was formed before Luke and Ethan concluded a contract. If the manner in which Aurora accepted is not within the contemplation of the offeror and is seen as more disadvantageous than how the offer was communicated, Luke and Aurora do not have a contract.

Key Cases

Adams v Lindsell [1818] *EWJC KB J59:* postal rule
Butler Machine Tool Co Ltd v Ex-cell-O Corporation Ltd [1979] 1 WLR 401 (CA): battle of the forms
Carlill v Carbolic Smoke Ball Company [1983] 1 QB 256: advertisements as an offer and unilateral offers
Dickinson v Dodds [1876] *2 Ch D 463*: revocation of offer by a reliable third party
Entores Ltd v Miles Far East Corp [1955] *2 QB 327*: acceptance takes place on receipt
Felthouse v Bindley [1862] *142 ER 1037*: silence does not constitute acceptance

Harvey v Face [1893] *AC 552:* request for information

Henthorn v Fraser [1892] *2 Ch 27* and *Re Household Fire Insurance v Grant* [1879] *4 Ex D 216:* qualification of the postal rule

Hyde v Wrench [1840] *3 Beav 334:* counteroffer destroys the offer

Matthieson Gee (Ayshire) Ltd v Quigley [1952] *UKHL 2*: inconsistency between offer and acceptance

Mondial Shipping and Chartering v Asarte Shipping Ltd [1995] *2 Lloyd's Rep 249:* acceptance takes place during normal business hours

Partridge v Crittenden [1968] *2 All ER 421:* advertisements as an invitation to treat

Payne v Cave [1789] 3 TR 148: auctions as invitation to treat

Pharmaceutical Society of Great Britain v Boots Cash Chemists [1953] 1 QB 401: display of goods in shop as an invitation to treat

Ramsgate Victoria Hotel v Montefiore [1866] *LR 1 Exch 109:* expiry of offer after a reasonable period

Routledge v Grant [1828] *4 Bing 653:* offer can be revoked before acceptance

Spencer v Harding [1870] LR 5 CP 561: tender as an invitation to treat

Stevenson v Mclean [1880] *5 QBD 346*: distinguishing counteroffer from request for further information

Storer v Manchester CC [1974] *1 WLR 1403:* intention to make an offer

Tenax Steamship Co v Owners of the Motor Vessel Brimnes [1974] *EWCA Civ 15 (The Brimnes)*: communication of acceptance

Tinn v Hoffman [1873] *29 LT 271*: cross offers

CHAPTER III

INTENTIONS TO CREATE LEGAL RELATIONS & CERTAINTY

Learning Outcomes:

After reading this chapter, you should be able to understand:

- ✓ What intention to create legal relations is;
- ✓ How the law distinguishes between social/domestic and commercial relations;
- ✓ Why courts cannot enforce an agreement that is too vague or incomplete;
- ✓ How certainty and intention to create legal relations are linked.

Questions and Answers:

INTENTION TO CREATE LEGAL RELATIONS

1. What is meant with intention to create legal relations?

In order to understand whether there is a binding contract it is necessary to establish what ***the intentions of the parties were at the time of contracting.***

People often make an agreement without necessarily intending for this to be legally binding. Sometimes it is very clear what the parties intend. An example would be if Sasha asks Alia if she wants to go the swimming pool together next week and Alia agrees. It is clear that neither Sasha nor Alia intents to create a legally binding agreement and that if one of the two cancels the arranged outing, the other would not be able to sue for breach of contract.

Other situations are more complex. For instance, Tam sees Oliver, Tam's neighbour, painting his fence and Tam asks Oliver if he would be willing to also paint Tam's fence in exchange for £30. Oliver agrees, but later decides he does not have time to paint Tam's fence. This arrangement seems more formal than Alia and Sasha's agreement to go swimming. However, did Tam and Oliver really intend to create a legally binding agreement? Should Tam now be able to sue Oliver for breach of contract?

The law presumes that in certain situations the parties intent for their agreement to be legally binding and in other situations the law presumes that the parties do not have this intention.

It is important to understand what the intention of the parties is because one of the main underlying principles of contract law is freedom of contract. Therefore, we need to establish whether the parties actually intended to enter into a contract. If they did not have the intention to create legal relations, then they have not agreed to take on the obligations flowing from the agreement. It would run counter to freedom of contract to enforce an agreement that the parties did not intended to be enforceable.

The intention of the parties is measured at ***the moment of concluding the contract***. The parties might change their mind subsequently, but for the law what counts is their intention at the time they made the agreement.

2. What is the presumption in commercial relations?

The presumption is that the parties do intent to create legal relations. Businesses want certainty and predictability. Businesses need to be able to count on the fact that an agreement they have entered into will be enforced.

The presumption is rebuttable, but the threshold for such a rebuttal is high in commercial relations (***Esso Petroleum Ltd v Commissioners of Custom and Excise [1976]***). One way the presumption can be rebutted is if ***the parties have expressly excluded that they intended to create legal relations*** (***Rose and Frank Co v JR Crompton and Bros Ltd [1925]***).

The context of the agreement is important when interpreting the language used by the parties. An employer promised his employees an ex-gratia payment and later went back on this promise by claiming he was not legally bound because of the wording 'ex gratia.' The court held there was an intention to create legal relations based on the context in which the promise was made, and the term 'ex-gratia' merely indicated that there was no pre-existing liability to pay before the agreement was concluded (***Edwards v Skyway [1964]***).

3. What is the presumption in domestic and social agreements?

The presumption is that the parties do not intend to create legal relations. The law recognises that in social situations most agreements are not intended to be binding.

The presumption is rebuttable, and the threshold of evidence required to prove the opposite is lower than in commercial relations. This is because it is far more likely that in a domestic/social situation the parties intended to create legal relations, than it is that in a commercial situation the parties did not intend to create legal relations.

An example of when the presumption was rebutted is ***Simpkins v Pays [1955]*** where the plaintiff was the lodger of the defendant. Each week, the plaintiff, the defendant, and the grandson of the defendant entered a competition in a newspaper. They agreed to share any winnings. They always entered under the name of the defendant and shared the entry fee and postage. When they won a price, the defendant refused to pay the plaintiff her share. The defendant stated there was no intention to create legal relations, but the court disagreed because through sharing the costs the parties had rebutted the presumption: *"This was in the nature of a very informal syndicate so that they could all get the benefit of success"* (Sellers J.).

This can be contrasted with ***Wilson v Burnett [2007]*** where a group of friends went to play bingo and made an agreement that if one of them won, they would share the price. One of the friends won but she refused to share her winnings and said that there was no intention to create legal relations. The court agreed as this arrangement had *'not crossed that line which exists between talk and meaning business or intention to create legal relations.'* A difference with ***Simpkins v Pay*** was that in that case there was a long-standing arrangement where the parties shared the costs of entering the competition.

4. How is the intention to create legal relations assessed?

The intention of the parties should be assessed objectively based on the facts available in each case (***Dresdner Kleinwort Ltd v Attrill [2013]***). If one of the parties knows that the other party does not intent to create legal relations, he is not entitled to assert that the other party did intend to create legal relations, and vice versa.

5. What case recognised the importance of the intention to create legal relations?

The seminal case of ***Balfour v Balfour [1919]*** established the doctrine of intention to create legal relations. Mrs and Mr Balfour married in 1900 and moved to Sri Lanka. They returned to England in 1915 as Mr Balfour was on leave. After his leave he returned to Sri Lanka, but Mrs Balfour stayed in England on advice of her doctor. The couple made an oral agreement according to which he promised to pay her £30 a month until she returned to Sri Lanka. In 1918 Mrs Balfour initiated divorce proceedings and sought to enforce the agreement regarding the £30 a month. The Court of Appeal held that Mr Balfour was not liable to continue to pay this sum, as there had been no intention to create legal relations given this was simply a domestic agreement between a married couple.

The Court of Appeal established the need to have the intention to create legal relations: "*It is necessary to remember that there are agreements between parties which do not result in contracts within the meaning of that term in our law. The ordinary example is where two parties agree to take a walk together, or where there is an offer and acceptance of hospitality*" (Atkin LJ.)

6. How does the presumption not to create legal relations works with family relations?

The presumption there is no intention to create legal relations applies to ***partners, if they are living in amity***.

In ***Balfour v Balfour*** the couple was living in amity when they made the arrangement that Mrs Balfour would receive £30 every month. When they separated Mrs Balfour could therefore not rely upon an arrangement made in happier times as there was a presumption, they did not intend to create legal relations at the time they made the arrangement.

In ***Meritt v Meritt [1970]*** an agreement between a husband and wife was enforceable because they agreed on the arrangement when they were separating: *"It is altogether different when the parties are not living in amity, but are separated, or about to separate. They then bargain keenly. They do not rely on honourable understandings. They want everything cut and dried. It may safely be presumed that they intend to create legal relations"* (Lord Denning).

The law thus distinguishes between agreements made between partners who are together and those that are no longer together or are in the process of separating.

The presumption that there is no intention to create legal relations also ***applies in other family relations***, such as parents and children (***Jones v Padavatton [1969]***). Do remember that the presumption is rebuttable and if it is proven there was an intention to create legal relations, the contract will be enforced by the court.

7. How can the presumption that the parties did not intent to create legal relations be rebutted?

This depends on the context in which the agreement was concluded and the individual circumstances of the case.

Some instances where the courts have rebutted the presumption:

- Where the parties have agreed to *share the ownership or tenancy of certain assets* such as a house, bank accounts, or finances (***Granatino v Radmacher [2010]***).
- Where the relationship between the parties is on the point of breaking down (***Meritt v Meritt [1970]***).
- Where an agreement between friends is concluded in a commercial context (***Snelling v John Snelling Ltd [1973]***).

The presumption can also be rebutted if one of the parties acted to their detriment in reliance upon the agreement. In ***Parker v Clark [1960]***, Mrs and Mr Parker agreed to move in with Mrs and Mr Clark. The plaintiffs agreed to share expenses of the household and the defendants agreed to leave their house to the plaintiffs when they died. The Parkers sold their home in reliance upon this agreement and moved in with the Clarks. Relationships deteriorated after they moved in and subsequently the Parkers moved out and brought an action for damages against the Clarks. The Clarks alleged that this was a domestic arrangement and there had been no intention to create legal relations. The court disagreed as the seriousness of the arrangement was demonstrated by the Parkers acting in reliance upon the agreement when they sold their house and therefore had nowhere else to live.

8. What is the role of letters of comfort and letters of intent?

The terms letters of comfort and letters of intent are often used interchangeably. They are ***letters used in commercial relations which indicate a willingness of the parties to enter into a contract***. To that purpose, they are often quite vague as to the concrete intentions of the parties and indicate more a general intention and willingness.

These letters are used ***to build trust*** between the parties in contractual negotiations and give clarity as to where they expect negotiations to go. Letters of comfort are often used to assure a contracting party that specific resources needed from a third party (bank, subsidiary) will be provided. They can also be used by a contracting party to encourage a third party to give them a loan as it shows there is a forthcoming contract that will provide resources to pay the third party back.

Do these letters also indicate an intention to create legal relations? The fact that a letter exists is not enough to indicate this, it depends on how concrete the content of the letter is and what it says about the intention of the parties (***Kleinwort Benson Ltd v Malaysia Mining Corp Bhd [1989]***). Such letters will often contain phrases such as ***'subject to contract'*** which make it clear that the parties do not intent this letter to be a binding agreement. However, if the wording of the letter of intent is concrete enough it can be binding.

CERTAINTY OF AGREEMENT

1. What do we mean with certainty of agreement?

Even if the parties have come to an agreement and intended to create legal relationships, their contract might not be certain enough to enforce. ***The agreement could be vague or incomplete on certain key points.*** If that is the case the court might not enforce the agreement.

For instance, if Tara and Juan have agreed that Tara will sell her canoe to Juan, but they have not agreed on a price and on a method and date of delivery it would be quite difficult to enforce the agreement if Juan later refuses to buy the canoe. Even if the judge is convinced that Juan and Tara intended to create legal relations, the judge might still decide there is no contract because without the crucial information of price, date, and delivery it is not possible to enforce the agreement.

The law gives effect to the agreements between parties, but the parties have to make the contract. The courts will interpret the contract and fill some of the gaps, but ***the courts will not write the contract.*** If the agreement is not sufficiently certain there is no contract.

2. Does this mean the parties have to agree on everything in advance?

No, this is not necessary. The contract has to be sufficiently certain, but ***the parties do not have to agree on every detail in advance.***

Contract law plays an important role in filling the gaps in the contract. If the parties have not made certain provisions, the court will use the law to fill in the gaps in the contract. ***Many contract law rules are variable.*** They have a backup function: If the parties have not made a decision on a specific issue, the court uses the law to fill in the gap on that issue.

The court interprets the contract and applies the law to the contract but will only enforce the contract if there is sufficient certainty of agreement.

3. What is the difference between curable and incurable incomplete agreements?

If curable the contract can be interpreted and constructed so as to give effect to the will of the parties and the contract is enforceable.

If incurable the contract cannot be interpreted and constructed so as to give effect to the will of the parties and the contract is not enforceable.

Scammell and Nephew v Ouston [1941] concerned a hire-purchase agreement. The defendants agreed to purchase a new van from Scammell *'on the understanding that the balance of the purchase price can be had on hire purchase terms over a period of two years.'* The court held that the agreement was too vague to be enforceable because it did not contain any details (such as the number of instalments and how hire-purchase should be defined under the contract). There was nothing that indicated the intentions of the parties and there is no overall accepted legal definition of what a hire-purchase contract is. If the court had enforced the agreement, it would have needed to draft the terms for the parties.

4. When is uncertain too uncertain?

There are no general rules on when an agreement is too uncertain or too vague to enforce. It depends on the context in which the agreement was made, if there is any other evidence from which the court can infer the intentions of the parties, whether there was any previous dealing between the parties, and on which specific issues the parties have not agreed. If these issues are details which do not go to the core of the agreement, the court can enforce the contract. If these issues go to the core of the agreement, usually the court will not enforce the agreement.

The courts are wary of parties introducing ***meaningless phrases*** into the contract, which would allow that party to escape the contract on the basis of uncertainty because it is unclear what is meant by that phrase. Therefore, ***if an uncertain phrase or clause can be deleted and there is still a workable contract***, the courts will ignore that phrase or clause.

In ***Nicolene v Simmonds [1953]*** the contract stated that "*We are in agreement that the usual conditions of acceptance apply.*" However, there were no usual conditions of acceptance nor was there any information on what these conditions were. The court therefore held this to be a meaningless phrase which did not affect whether the contract could be enforced.

5. What happens if performance of the contract has already started?

Courts are more likely to decide there is an enforceable agreement once performance has started. This is because ***performance gives an indication on how the agreement should be interpreted.***

Course of dealing and trade usages help clarify the intentions of the parties. In ***Hillas & Co. Ltd v Arcos Ltd [1932]*** the parties made a contract for the supply of timber of *'fair specification.'* While it is unclear what fair means, the court could determine the meaning because of previous dealings between the parties which included the same clause. Furthermore, as the parties were professionals in the timber trade, they would have understood what fair specification meant.

It can happen that even though ***performance has already started that there is no legally binding agreement*** because the contract is incomplete. Two companies made an agreement for the delivery of building materials. They did not agree on important issues such as manner of delivery and price. Nevertheless, the seller claimants delivered some of the items. After a dispute broke out the claimants wanted a fair price for the items they delivered and the defendants counter-claimed for non-delivery of the remaining items. The court held that despite the part performance there was no contract because the parties had not agreed on key issues. The claimants were allowed to recover damages on a *quantum meruit* (what one has earned) basis for work performed (***British Steel Corporation v Cleveland Bridge and Engineering Co. Ltd [1984]***).

6. Is it always necessary to include a price in the contract?

Courts can enforce contracts which do not stipulate a price. ***If a price has not been agreed between the parties, 'a reasonable price' should be paid.*** Deciding on the reasonable price is a question of fact and is decided by looking at the average market price for comparable goods and services.

This approach is found in *the Supply of Goods and Services Act 1982* (Section 15), *the Consumer Rights Act 2015* (Section 52), and the *Sale of Goods Act 1979* (Section 8).

7. How can uncertainty be solved through a machinery?

A machinery is what we call ***a mechanism that is included in the contract to resolve an aspect which is uncertain.*** For instance, the parties might include a clause that says the exchange rate of the currency will be determined by bank X on date Y or a clause that says the price will be decided by an independent valuer.

The contract would then not be seen as uncertain or too vague because the parties have included in their contract the means to resolve this uncertainty. In ***Sudbrook Trading Estate v Eggleton [1982]*** the parties agreed that the price for the exercise of an option to purchase was to be determined by two valuers, one nominated by each party. One of the parties refused to nominate a valuer and said that the contract was void because of uncertainty. The House of Lords held that the contract included a machinery through which the price could be determined and was thus not uncertain.

8. How is the law on uncertainty evolving?

As noted, there are very few general rules on certainty.

In ***May and Butcher Ltd v The King [1934]*** the government made a contract to sell surplus tents to May and Butcher Ltd. The company paid a security deposit for the tents. The written agreement stated that the price and date of payment would be decided later. The government changed their mind and no longer wanted to sell the tents. The company sued and the House of Lords decided that there was no legally binding agreement between the parties because fundamental terms had not been agreed.

This case represents ***a restrictive approach to certainty*** and does not take into account the intentions of the parties to form legal relations. It is clear from both the deposit and the written agreement that the parties intended to form legal relations.

The law is evolving in a direction that places ***paramount importance on the intentions of the parties to form legal relations*** as expressed by Blanchard Justice: *"No longer should it be said that … if something essential is left to be agreed upon by the parties at a later time, there is no binding agreement. The intention of the parties, as discerned by the court, to be bound or not be bound should be paramount"* (***Fletcher Challenge Energy Ltd v Electricity Corporation of New Zealand Ltd [2002]***). This reflects the *favor contractus* principle which means that in contractual disputes the courts should favour upholding the agreement because this best reflects the intention of the parties and it is usually in the interest of both parties to keep the contract alive, even if the contract is deficient. If the contract is declared void the parties would usually need to source alternative goods and services which costs extra time and money. This is a principle of transnational contract law as reflected by the UNIDROIT Principles of International Commercial Contracts and the Convention for Contracts for the International Sale of Goods.

This less restricted approach gives the court a larger role in deciding the terms of the contract and makes the interpretation of the contract more subjective (because the court will fill the gaps in the contract). The court must find a balance between the intentions of the parties to create legal relations and the difficulties of enforcing an incomplete agreement.

Summary:

- For an agreement to be enforceable the parties must have intended to create legal relations.
- In domestic and social agreements there is a presumption that the parties did not intend to create legal relations.
- In a commercial agreement there is a presumption that the parties did intend to create legal relations.
- Both presumptions are rebuttable, but in commercial agreements there is a high threshold to rebutting the presumption.
- Not all details of the contract can be arranged in advance. This is also not necessary because the courts can interpret the contract through the law, course of dealing, custom and trade usages.
- If key issues have not been decided and the agreement is too vague or incomplete, the contract could be declared void because of lack of certainty. Whilst the court can interpret the contract, it will not write the contract for the parties.

Problem Question:

Ruben is a carpenter and Tyler is a cabinetmaker. They are also good friends. One day they decide that it will be cheaper if they buy timber together. They do this successfully for a year. There is no real pattern to this, they sometimes go together to buy the timber, sometimes one of them goes and they split the timber later. They go sometimes once a month, but other times it might be every 2 weeks. They do not always split the timber 50/50 as it depends on their needs. After a year Ruben sources even cheaper timber, but the quantities they sell are much smaller, so he does not want to share with Tyler. He tells Tyler that they do not have a contract anyway and from now on he will buy his own timber. Tyler wants some legal advice on the situation.

1) Was there an intention to create legal relations?
2) Was there certainty of agreement?

Ruben and Tyler are good friends so this would indicate that there is a presumption that there was no intention to create legal relations (***Balfour v Balfour [1919]***). However, the dealings took place in the course of their respective businesses which would likely be enough to rebut the presumption (***Snelling v John Snelling Ltd [1973]***). Therefore, it could be decided that they did intend to create legal relations.

Ruben and Tyler did not agree on the details of their contract which might mean it is too vague or uncertain to be enforced (***Scammell and Nephew v Ouston [1941]***). As performance already started the court could take into account course of dealing to fill in the gaps of the contract (***Hillas & Co. Ltd v Arcos Ltd [1932]***). In this case this might not be enough as no clear pattern was established. This could lead the court to decide that there is no contract because it would be difficult to fill in the gaps of the contract based on course of dealing. It could also be that the court decides that each individual transaction was a contract but that there is no overall agreement because the terms were too vague (***Baird Textiles Holdings Ltd v Marks & Spencer plc [2001]***). It is not clear what the terms of the agreement are with regards to amount and frequency. Therefore, it could be held that there was no overall agreement because of uncertainty.

Key Cases

Baird Textiles Holdings Ltd v Marks & Spencer plc [2001] *EWCA Civ 274:* each transaction is an individual contract, no overall agreement

Balfour v Balfour [1919] *2 KB 571*: intention to create legal relations are necessary to establish there is a contract & no intention for couples living in amity

Dresdner Kleinwort Ltd v Attrill [2013] EWCA Civ 394: objective assessment

Jones v Padavatton [1969] *1 WLR 328*: contracts between parents and children

Meritt v Meritt [1970] *EWCA Civ 6*: contracts between a couple that is separating

Parker v Clark [1960] *1 WLR 286:* party acting in reliance on agreement

Rose and Frank Co v JR Crompton and Bros Ltd [1925] *AC 445:* excluding an agreement from being legally binding

Simpkins v Pays [1955] *1 WLR 1975*: rebutting the presumption in social contracts.

British Steel Corporation v Cleveland Bridge and Engineering Co. Ltd [1984]1 All ER 504: Performance has started but no contract

Hillas & Co. Ltd v Arcos Ltd [1932] *UKHL 2:* Course of dealing and trade usages

May and Butcher Ltd v The King [1934] 2 KB 17: classic approach to certainty

Nicolene v Simmonds [1953] *1 QB 543*: meaningless phrases do not stop enforcement

Scammell and Nephew v Ouston [1941] *AC 251*: Contract cannot be enforced if too vague or uncertain

CHAPTER IV

CONSIDERATION & PROMISSORY ESTOPPEL

Learning Outcomes:

After reading this chapter, you should be able to understand:

- ✓ What consideration is;
- ✓ That consideration should be sufficient but need to not be adequate, that it can be executory or executed but cannot be past;
- ✓ Why performing an existing duty is no consideration and how going beyond an existing duty is consideration;
- ✓ How promissory estoppel works in relation to consideration.

Questions and Answers:

1. What is consideration?

For a contract to be enforceable it needs to be supported by consideration. It means that both parties should get something of value out of the contract. It is a ***quid for pro quo*** approach. For an offer to be legally binding the promisor must seek something in return from the promisee. The promisor is the person who makes the promise and the promisee is the person to whom the promise is made.

Example: Daniel sells his computer to Adam for £300. Adam gets a computer and Daniel gets £300. Therefore, they both get something out of the contract.

Gratuitous promises are in principle not enforceable.

Example: Daniel promises Adam to give him his computer. Daniel later changes his mind and decides to keep the computer. Adam likely cannot force Daniel to give him the computer because he did not provide consideration to Daniel and thus there is no enforceable contract. This is called a ***nudum pactum*** (a bare promise). However, such a promise is enforceable when the agreement is contained in a ***deed*** (a document under seal).

2. How is consideration defined?

The classic definition is: *"a valuable consideration in the sense of the law, may consist either in some right, interest, profit or benefit accruing to one party, or some forbearance, detriment, loss or responsibility given, suffered or undertaken by the other."*

(***Currie v Misa [1875]***).

This definition proved problematic because in practice there is no benefit or detriment for the parties until contract is performed.

Example: When Daniel offers to sell his computer to Adam for £300 and Adam agrees, neither Adam nor Daniel benefits from the agreement until performance. Only when the contract is performed both suffer a loss (giving up the computer or giving up money) and both gain a benefit (gaining money or gaining a computer).

Modern contract law sees consideration as ***the price of the promise***. This was defined by Sir Frederick Pollock as follows: *"An act or forbearance of one party, or the promise thereof, is the price for which the promise of the other is bought, and the promise thus given for value is enforceable."*[2] This definition was approved by the House of Lords in ***Dunlop Pneumatic Tyre Co. Ltd v Selfridge and Co. Ltd [1915].***

Consideration should be asked for.

Example: Daniel gives Adam his computer. Adam is very happy and gives Daniel £300 in return. This is not consideration as Daniel never asked for the money. This means there is no enforceable contract. This is important because if the computer does not work properly Adam cannot sue Daniel for breach of contract. There is no contract between them after all.

3. What are the different types of consideration?

1. *Executory* – a mutual exchange of promises.
2. *Executed* – a promise in exchange for the performance of an act.
3. *Past consideration* – the act is performed before the promise is made (not valid consideration).

Example executory consideration:

Daniel promises to sell his computer to Adam and Adam promises to pay £300 for the computer. They decide that Adam will pay next Tuesday, and Daniel will deliver the computer next Wednesday. The parties have exchanged promises, but performance of the contract is in the future. The consideration is executory.

Example executed consideration:

Daniel promises to sell his computer to Adam and Adam promises to pay £300 for the computer. Adam gives Daniel the money immediately. Daniel promises

---

[2] Frederick Pollock, Principles of Contract Law: a treatise on the general principles concerning the validity of agreements in the law of England, 8th edition, London Stevens and Sons, 1911, p. 175.

to deliver the computer next week. Adam has now executed his consideration, but Daniel's consideration remains executory.

Consideration in unilateral contracts is executed:

Jiya promises £1,000 for anyone that finds her dog. Sabrina finds Jiya's dog and returns it. By finding Jiya's dog, Sabrina has executed the consideration for the promise.

4. What about past consideration?

Past consideration is no consideration. If a promise is made after performance, it is not consideration.

Example: Daniel gives Adam his computer. Adam promises that he will give Daniel £300 next week. Adam changes his mind and decides not give Daniel the money. Daniel is upset and wants to sue Adam for breach of contract. However, there was no exchange of a promise for an act. Daniel did not ask for the money beforehand and he already gave the computer to Adam before Adam made his promise. Therefore, there was no consideration for Adam's promise to pay £300.

In the case of ***Eastwood v Kenyon [1840]*** Sarah's father died, and she inherited from him. Mr Eastwood was Sarah's guardian as she was underage when her father passed away. Mr Eastwood borrowed £140 to pay for Sarah's education. When Sarah grew up, she married Mr Kenyon. Mr Kenyon promised to discharge Mr Eastwood's debt because he had taken good care of Sarah. He then changed his mind. The court held that Mr Kenyon had the right to go back on his promise because Mr Eastwood's consideration (taking care of Sarah) was not in return for Mr Kenyon's promise as it was already performed before Mr Kenyon made the promise.

There is an exception to this rule. ***Past consideration is sufficient if provided at the promisor's request and if there is an (implicit) understanding between the parties that payment will be made in return for the act.***

In ***Lampleigh v Brathwait [1615]*** the defendant was imprisoned for murder. In order to be acquitted he needed a pardon from the King. He therefore asked Mr Lampleigh to obtain such a pardon for him. Mr Lampleigh got the pardon for Mr Brathwait, although this cost him time and money. When he got the pardon, Mr Brathwait promised to pay £100 to Mr Lampleigh. He didn't pay so Mr Lampleigh went to court. The court held that the service was performed at the request of the defendant and there was an implicit understanding between the two men that this service would not be for free. Therefore, the consideration was sufficient.

This exception was later considered in some detail in ***Pa On v Lau Yiu Long [1980]*** by Lord Scarman who developed the following test:

1) Is the act performed at the request of the promisor?
2) Did the parties understand that something would be expected in return for the act?
3) Would the promised benefit be enforceable as consideration if promised in advance?

If the answer to these questions is yes, then past consideration is sufficient.

Example: if you take a taxi to the airport, you might not discuss the price in advance and maybe will not even mention payment to the driver. When you arrive at the airport the driver will tell you the price. You cannot refuse to pay the driver on account of his consideration being past. There is an implicit understanding between you and the taxi driver that of course he would not drive you there for free and that you will owe him payment for the service.

(Other exceptions include bills of exchange (See Section 27 Bills of Exchange Act 1882) and previous debts for capital gain tax purposes (See Section 29(5) of the Limitations Act 1980)).

5. What does it mean that consideration must be sufficient?

Consideration should be sufficient, but it need not be adequate. Sufficient means that something in value must be given as consideration for a promise. However, the value does not need to be adequate. This means that the bargain does not need to be a good bargain.

Example: if Daniel's computer is worth £300 but he agrees with Adam to sell it to him for £25 then the consideration (£25) is sufficient (as £25 has value) but not adequate (as the computer is worth £300).

The parties decide what bargain they want to make and how much they are willing to pay for something. If Daniel later realises that he could have gotten much more for his computer and that he made a very bad bargain, he cannot change his mind. ***The law does not protect people from making bad bargains.***

Whether consideration is sufficient depends on the circumstances, and something which might not have any objective value can be good consideration. In ***Chapell & Co Ltd v The Nestlé Co Ltd [1960]*** the claimants owned the copyright of a song. The defendants wanted to supply a record which included this song to everyone that would send a postal order for 1s 6d and three wrappers from Nestlé chocolate bars. There was a dispute over how much royalties should be paid. Nestlé said that the wrappers were not part of the consideration because the wrappers were worthless. The House of Lords held that the wrappers were not worthless to Nestlé because they represented sold chocolate bars from which the company had profited. The wrappers were therefore part of the consideration.

6. What is nominal consideration?

Nominal consideration is ***a symbolic sum*** such as £1. It is mainly meant to ensure that there is an enforceable bargain between the parties. P. Atiyah: "*a promise for nominal consideration is just about the clearest possible indication that the promisor intended his promise seriously and intended to give the promise a legally enforceable right.*"[3]

The image of a ***peppercorn*** is often used to symbolize the principles on the sufficiency of consideration: This is a tangible object and has some (albeit very minimal) value, and therefore would be sufficient (but certainly not adequate in the vast majority of contracts).

7. What do we mean with that to be sufficient consideration must have some value?

There must be some ***economic value*** attached to the consideration. In ***Chappell v Nestlé [1960]*** the chocolate wrappers were intrinsically worthless, but they did represent a value to Nestlé because it meant that they had sold more chocolate as people wanted the record.

In ***Thomas v Thomas [1842]*** a husband promised his wife that she could stay living in the house after he died. The executors of the estate agreed to accept £1 in rent a year. The payment was not adequate, but it was sufficient because there is economic value in the £1.

This value does not necessarily need to be a monetary value but can also be a service or other benefit (***Bainbridge v Firmstone [1880]***).

Giving up a worthless claim and a promise not to sue can be sufficient consideration (***Cook v Wright [1861]***). In this case the tenant of a house received a notice saying that he was responsible for contributing to the costs of work being done in the adjacent street. The defendant did not think he needed to pay because he was only a tenant and not the owner of the house. The

[3] P. Atiya, 'Consideration: A Restatement' in *Essays on Contract*, Oxford University Press, 1986, p. 194.

plaintiffs threatened him with legal action unless he contributed. The defendant offered to pay a reduced contribution in three instalments in return for the plaintiffs not suing him. The plaintiffs agreed but the defendant only paid the first instalment. The plaintiffs sued him for the remaining two instalments. The court stated that the defendant was right that he did not have to contribute because he was not the owner, but that the promise of the plaintiffs they would not sue in return for the reduced contribution was sufficient consideration because a court case costs considerable time and money which the defendant would have been spared if he had made the payment. Therefore, the promise of the defendant to pay was enforceable, even if in the first place the defendant had no responsibility to pay.

If the claim is worthless a promise not to sue only amounts to sufficient consideration if the person making the claim is not aware that the claim is worthless. Otherwise, it would be very easy to take advantage and put pressure on the other person by threatening to sue them. So, ***the person making the promise should think they have a genuine claim.***

The promise should also be asked for. In ***Combe v Combe [1951]*** a husband and wife divorced, and the husband promised her an annual allowance which he later did not pay. The wife then sued him and said that her consideration was that she had not exercised her right to apply for maintenance. Whilst giving up such a right could be sufficient consideration; in this case it was not because the husband had not asked her not to apply for maintenance.

Therefore:

- There must be a genuine belief that there is a claim.
- There must be a genuine intention to bring legal proceedings (no empty threats).
- There should be a clear promise not to sue in return for x
- This promise should be asked for.

8. So, when is consideration not sufficient?

There are no general rules for this, and it depends on the facts of the case. In most transactions the consideration is easy to find. There should at least be some ***material value*** to the consideration.

A father promised his son that he would not sue him for the money the son had borrowed from him. The son in return promised his father not to bore him with his endless complaints. The court decided that the promise of the son not to complain was not sufficient consideration because, there was no material value to this (***White v Bluett [1853]***).

It should also be clear that ***a promise to do something illegal or refrain from doing something illegal*** can never be sufficient consideration.

Example: John promises Mary £5,000 if she steals a car for him. Mary does so. John now refuses to pay. John's promise is not enforceable.

Mary promises not to break into John's house if he gives her £5,000. John says yes, but later changes his mind. John's promise is not enforceable.

9. Who can enforce the promise?

A person can only enforce a promise if they can show that they have provided consideration for that promise. ***Consideration must move from the promisee*** (***Price v Easton [1833]***).

Whilst consideration must move from the promisee, ***it does not necessarily need to move to the promisor.*** In ***Tweddle v Atkinson [1861]*** two young people were getting married. The father of the groom and the father of the bride agreed that they would pay respectively £100 and £200 in consideration for the marriage. The father of the bride died before he could pay the £200. The groom sued his father-in-law's estate for the money. His action failed, because he had provided no consideration, even if he was the beneficiary of the contract. The only person that could sue would be father of the groom because he had provided consideration, even if he was not the beneficiary of the contract.

Note: The law has now significantly changed with the Contract (Rights of Third Parties) Act 1999 (See Chapter V).

If someone is a party to the contract but has provided no consideration themselves, they would still be entitled to benefit from the contract as ***a joined promisee*** (***Coulls v Bagot's Executor and Trustee Ltd [1967]***).

10. Is the performance of an existing legal duty consideration?

An act which a person is legally obliged to perform is not consideration (***Collins v Godefroy [1831]***). In the above case the plaintiff was summoned to give evidence in court and the defendant promised to pay him for this service. The plaintiff gave evidence and the defendant refused to pay. The court held that there was no consideration because the plaintiff was legal obliged to give evidence anyway. The plaintiff had done nothing extra than he already had to do and therefore had not provided any consideration.

However, if someone goes ***above and beyond their legal duty*** this can be consideration and the contract would be enforceable (***Glasbrook Brothers v***

Glamorgan County Council [1925]). In this case the owners of a mine were worried about a strike turning violent and they asked the police if they could station a garrison outside the mine. The police assessed the situation and did not think this was necessary. The owners promised to pay the police if they did station the garrison. The police agreed. There was no violence and the owners refused to pay the police. The House of Lords held that consideration was provided because whilst the police have a legal duty to maintain law and order, the police had judged this situation did not warrant a stationed garrison, and by agreeing to do something which they did not deem necessary the police had gone beyond their legal duty and were thus entitled to payment.

The performance of the extra act should be at the request of the promisor, it should not be required by law, and is deemed unnecessary by the authorities. ***If the act of the promisor causes the risk to occur*** **and the need for the public duty to be performed** this would also be sufficient consideration (***Harris v Sheffield United Football Club [1988]***).

A controversial case is that of ***Ward v Byham [1956]*** where a man and a woman had an illegitimate child. Mr Byham promised Ms Ward that he would provide maintenance for the child if she made sure the child was looked after and happy. Mr Byham did not pay and under the law at the time he had no legal duty to pay maintenance for an illegitimate child. Mr Byham argued that there was no consideration for his promise to pay maintenance because Ms Ward was already legally obliged to look after her child. The court held that consideration was provided because whilst Ms Ward indeed had a legal duty to look after her child, her promise to make the child happy went beyond her duty and was sufficient consideration.

The court considered something intangible like happiness to be sufficient consideration. Whilst there is certainly a lot of value in happiness, it is also difficult to define, and it would be problematic to judge whether the child was really happy. It is clear that the court wanted to achieve a just result for Ms Ward and therefore interpreted the sufficiency of consideration in a broader way.

11. Is the performance of an existing contractual duty to a third-party consideration?

Yes, if one party has an existing contractual duty then the performance of that duty can be consideration in relation to a third party. Mr Scotson contracted with X to supply a load of coal to X or to anyone that X nominated. X nominated Mr Pegg. Mr Pegg did not unload the coal and claimed he had no contractual duty to do so. The court held that delivery of the coal was consideration for unloading the coal. Scotson already owed delivery to X, but that was irrelevant in Scotson's dealings with Pegg (***Scotson v Pegg [1861]***).

12. Is consideration necessary for modifying the contract?

Yes, ***the modification of the contract requires consideration.***

The parties can do two things:

1) End the existing contract and make a new contract (*Watkins & Sons Inc v Carrig [1941]*)
2) Ensure the change is supported by consideration on both sides.

The parties can make an agreement to end the contract. If both of the parties still have any duties left, the consideration would be the mutual release from duties.

If only one the parties still has duties left, then there is no consideration for the other party releasing them from their duty. In that case it would be advisable to ensure that there is some type of consideration for this release (which could be nominal consideration).

13. Is the performance of an existing contractual duty owed to the promisor sufficient consideration?

This situation occurs when the contract is modified, but only benefits one of the parties.

Example: Aziza has asked Simon to build a conservatory in her garden. In return Aziza agrees to pay £10,000 to Simon. Simon starts work on the conservatory, but soon realises it was more work than he anticipated. He asks Aziza for an addition £5,000. Aziza agrees to pay this. Once the conservatory is finished, Aziza refuses to pay the additional £5,000. The question is if Simon is entitled to the additional money.

In the contract between Simon and Aziza it is easy to find the consideration. Simon gets £10,000 and Aziza gets a conservatory. However, when Aziza promises the extra £5,000 what is the consideration? She is getting a conservatory, but she was already getting that anyway under the original contract. She is getting nothing extra for her £5,000. Simon has not provided any consideration.

If the parties do go above their contractual duty this is consideration for the promise.

This issue was considered in the seminal case of ***Stilk v Myrick [1809]***. Halfway through a sea voyage two sailors deserted the ship. The captain promised the remaining sailors that if they worked the ship back to port, he would give the wages of the deserters to the remaining crew. Once the ship was back in port the carrier refused to honour that promise.

The court held that the promise was unenforceable because the crew had done nothing extra from what was in their contract. There was therefore no consideration for the captain's promise. Whilst obviously the crew had to work harder with fewer people on board this was not considered going beyond their duty. The public policy angle was also considered by the courts: by allowing for the promise to stand they feared that this would lead to opportunistic workers demanding extra wages for performing their contractual duty. The law reports on the case are conflicted on whether the lack of consideration or the public policy/duress angle was the primary motivation behind the court's decision.

The above case can be contrasted with ***Hartley v Ponsonby [1857]*** whereby the crew of a ship was promised extra wages after several crew members had deserted. The carrier refused to pay the extra wages. The court held that the promise of the additional payment was enforceable because the crew had exceeded their contractual duty.

Why did the court make a different decision in *Hartley*? The crucial difference was the number of sailors that had deserted the ship. In *Stilk* this was two out of 12 and in *Hartley* it was 19 out of 36 and therefore more than half the crew. Whilst the sailors would undoubtedly have had to work harder after two of the crew had abandoned the ship it did not represent a fundamental deviation from their contract. In *Hartley* not only did the crew have to work a lot harder and take on different tasks, but the journey also became a lot more dangerous with so few sailors. The circumstances under which they performed their contract were quite different from what they intended at the time of contracting and therefore the sailors had provided consideration.

14. How has the law on existing contractual duty changed?

The effects of ***Stilk v Myrick*** were limited by ***Williams v Roffey Bros & Nicholls (Contractors) Ltd [1990]*** which introduced the concept of a ***practical benefit as sufficient consideration***.

Roffey Bros contracted to build 27 new flats. Roffey Bros was under some time pressure to get the work done because their contract contained a penalty clause for late delivery. They subcontracted the carpentry work out to Williams in exchange for £20,000. Halfway through the work Williams asked for additional payment as they had miscalculated how much work it would be. Roffey Bros concerned with getting the work done promised an extra £575 per flat. In the end Williams completed eight of the flats and was only paid £1,500. Williams sued Roffey Bros for the outstanding money. The question was whether he was entitled to the extra payment. Given that the completion of the flats was an existing contractual duty, Williams did not seem to have provided any consideration in return for the additional pay.

The courts decided that Williams was entitled to the money because he had provided consideration in the form of a practical benefit. The quick completion of the work would have allowed Roffey Bros to escape the penalty clause and they would not have needed to find new carpenters. Both parties therefore benefited from the agreement.

Thus, if there is a contract between the parties, there are issues with performance and a promise of additional payment is made, if there was no fraud/duress, and ***a practical benefit can be found for the other party, the promise is enforceable.***

What exactly a practical benefit is remains rather vague, there should be some advantage for the other party, but it is unclear exactly what the limits are. ***Williams v Roffey Bros*** (Court of Appeal) does not overrule ***Stilk v Myrick*** (House of Lords) but qualifies the latter further. The exact relationship between the two cases is not settled yet.

15. What is the relationship between part-payment of debt and consideration?

This refers to a situation where A owes B money and B says that he will discharge the rest of the debt in return for a part-payment of the debt. A does not provide any consideration for this promise, and therefore it is not an enforceable contract and B can later go back on his word.

In ***Foakes v Beer [1884]*** Mr Foakes owed Mrs Beer a sum of £2,090. They made an agreement that he would pay her back over time, did not have to pay any interest, and Mrs Beer would not sue upon the debt. After Foakes paid back the debt Mrs Beer sued him for interest. The House of Lords held that the agreement was not supported by consideration because the payment of the debt itself did not constitute consideration for Mrs Beer's promise to forgo any interest. Mr Foakes already owed the money to Mrs Beer and did not give her anything extra in return for her promise.

For the part payment of the debt in satisfaction of the whole to be enforceable some consideration should be provided. This could be a different time or place of payment or the addition of something extra: *"Payment of a lesser sum on the day in satisfaction of a greater cannot be any satisfaction for the whole but a change in time or mode of payment, or the addition by the debtor of tomtit, a canary or the like will suffice to constitute consideration."*

(Sir Edward Coke ***(Pinnel's Case [1602]***).

Example: Dina owes Maya £1,000, and she needs to pay her a £200 a month. Dina is struggling to pay. Maya says to Dina she will take £500 instead of the £1,000 provided Dina gives her the money now. Dina has provided consideration because she is giving Maya the money immediately instead of at the time of the originally agreed instalments.

This new element should be introduced at the request of the creditor and there should be some benefit to the creditor, otherwise this could lead to a situation where the creditor is put under a lot of pressure to accept (***D&C Builders Ltd v Rees [1966]***).

Re Selectmove Ltd [1995] considered ***the principle of practical benefit in relation to part-payment of debt.*** This concerned a tax dispute whereby an alleged agreement was made between the company and HM Revenue and Customs (HMRC) regarding the recovery of outstanding taxes in instalments. HMRC demanded immediate payment and when this was not forthcoming sought to wound up the company. No consideration was provided for the agreement because Selectmove already owed the money to HMRC. Selectmove argued that its continued existence was a practical benefit for HMRC as if the company continued to exist and make money it was much more likely that the company would contribute more taxes in the long run. The Court of Appeal agreed that this would be a practical benefit but did not extent ***Williams v Roffey Bros*** to payment of debt as this would leave ***Foakes v Beer*** (a House of Lords decision) without any application.

In ***MWB Business Exchange Centes Ltd. v Rock Advertising Ltd [2018]*** the Supreme Court refrained from ruling on the issue because in the words of Lord Sumption: *"This was likely to involve a re-examination of the decision in* ***Foakes v Beer****. It is probably ripe for re-examination. But if it is to be overruled or its effect substantially modified, it should be before an enlarged panel of the court and in a case where the decision would be more than obiter dictum."*

It is therefore unclear how the law will evolve further. There are some exceptions to the rules on part-payment of debt:

1) ***Disputed claims*:** If the parties have a genuine dispute about whether the amount is actually owed or on the precise amount

that is owed– as the full debt is not known any amount is sufficient (*Cooper v Parker [1885]*).

2) ***Unliquidated claims***: The sum of money owed is uncertain and therefore any amount is sufficient.
3) ***Composition agreements***: The debtor owes money to different people and makes an agreement with the different creditors to pay a percentage of his debt to each creditor in satisfaction of the complete debt. This is binding because it would amount to fraud on all parties if one of the creditors could go back on the arrangement and sue for the remainder of the debt. Likely the debtor would not have enough money to pay everyone back, and the other creditors would not get the agreed for percentage. The creditors are bound in a contract and have a contractual duty to each other.
4) ***Payment by a third party*** (***Hirachand Punachand v Temple [1911]***): If a third person agrees to offer part-payment in satisfaction of the complete debt and the creditor agrees with this arrangement, he can later not go back on this and sue the debtor for the full amount.

- ***Example:*** Hermia owes Avery £700. Luna offers Avery £500 in settlement of Hermia's debt. Avery agrees to accept the £500. Avery cannot go back on this agreement and sue Hermia for the rest of the money.

16. What are the reasons we have consideration?

Consideration has an important ***evidentiary function***. If it is necessary to prove there was an agreement between the parties and that the parties intend this agreement to be binding, then consideration can prove that the parties were serious about their intent: "*The importance of consideration is that it is a valuable signal that the parties intend to be bound by their agreement, rather than an end in itself.*" (Baragwanath J in ***Antons Trawling Co Ltd v Smith [2002]***).

Consideration also helps the court to decide on damages to be awarded in case of breach of contract because it indicates to the court what the parties thought their contract was worth and ***what the measure of the obligation is***.

An argument against the requirement of consideration is that there are times when the courts significantly extend the interpretation of sufficient consideration ***to avoid a party from being able go back on his word if this would cause some form of injustice*** (such as in ***Ward v Byham***). If a peppercorn is sufficient consideration the benefit does not really add anything to the transaction but is merely introduced for the sake of having consideration.

This creates a certain artificiality in the contract whereby it is necessary to find consideration for the sake of there being consideration. ***It could defeat the intentions of the parties to be bound by the agreement***, if a failure of finding consideration means that there is no contract.

Civil law jurisdictions, mixed-law jurisdictions (including Scotland), and transnational commercial law instruments (such as the UNIDROIT Principles of International Commercial Contracts) do not require consideration for a contract to be enforceable. They ***focus on whether the parties have reached agreement and intended to create legal relations***. The existence of consideration is taken into account by the courts, but the absence of consideration does not mean there is no contract.

17. What is the relationship between promissory estoppel and consideration?

Promissory estoppel is ***a principle of equity that can, in certain circumstances, act as an exception to the rule that consideration is necessary for a contract to be enforceable***.

Promissory estoppel means that if A, by his words or actions, has led B to believe in a particular state of affairs, and B has relied on this state of affairs, A will not be allowed to go back on his words or actions when it would be unjust and inequitable for him to do so.

In ***Central London Property v High Trees House [1947]***, the plaintiff leased a block of flats to the defendant. The defendant had intended to sublet the flats but when World War II broke out people left London and it was difficult to find tenants. The plaintiff agreed to half the rent payable by the defendant. The defendant paid the reduced rent until 1945. After the war finished the flats were fully occupied again so the defendant could pay the original sum. The plaintiff sued for the recovery of the original rent for the last 2 quarters of 1945.

The defendant had provided no consideration for the promise of the plaintiff to half the rent. The court held that the plaintiff had made a promise which he intended to be binding and the defendant had acted upon that promise. Therefore, the plaintiff should be estopped from going back on his promise because it would be unequitable for him to do so. The plaintiff could claim for the full amount going forward, but not retrospectively go back on his promise.

The necessary elements of promissory estoppel are:

- A pre-existing legal relationship between the parties ***(Bairds v Marks & Spencer [2000])***;

- A clear and unequivocal promise **(Woodhouse AC Israel Cocoa SA v Nigerian Produce Marketing [1972]);**
- Evidence that the promisee has relied on that promise ***(Hughes v Metropolitan Railway [1877]),*** although this reliance does not need to be detrimental **(*The Post Chaser [1982]* and *WJ Alan & Co Ltd v El Nasr Export & Import Co [1972]*);**
- Unequitable for the promisor to go back on his promise;
- Estoppel suspends rights but does not extinguish them;
- Estoppel acts as a shield and not as a sword, it can be used as a defence to a claim, but not as a cause of action **(*Combe v Combe [1951]*).**

Promissory estoppel can apply in cases of part-payment of debt. In ***Collier v P&MJ Wright Holdings [2008]*** the defendant was owed a judgment debt of £46,800 by the claimant and his two partners. The partners went bankrupt, and the defendant sought to reclaim the complete sum from the claimant. The claimant relied on an agreement with the defendant that stated he only needed to pay part of the debt. The court held that part-payment of debt is not good consideration in satisfaction of a full debt, but that the creditors could be estopped from going back on their promise if this was unequitable.

Promissory estoppel should not be used to help a party who has behaved in an ***unconscionable or inequitable way***. From hence the adage that 'he who comes to equity should come with clean hands.'

In ***D&C Builders v Rees [1966]*** Mr and Mrs Rees contracted D&C Builders for some work. The plaintiffs were owed £482, 13s, and 1d. Mrs Rees knew that D&C Builders were experiencing financial difficulties and she offered them £300 in satisfaction of the debt. D&C Builders agreed, but they later sued to recover the balance. Mrs and Mr Rees argued that it would be inequitable for D&C Builders to go back on their promise. The court disagreed because of the behaviour of the defendants who knew that the plaintiffs had financial difficulties and had pressured them into agreeing. Danckwerts LJ: "*The Rees behaved very badly... I cannot see any ground in this case for treating the payment as a satisfaction on equitable principles.*"

Summary:

- For a contract to be binding there should be consideration, a gratuitous promise is only binding if contained in a deed.
- Consideration must be sufficient, but it need not be adequate.
- Consideration must move from the promisee… but not necessarily to the promisor.

- Consideration can be executory (an exchange of promises) or executed (a promise in exchange for an act).
- Past consideration is no consideration, except when the service is provided at the promisor's request and there is an implied understanding that some type of payment for the service would be forthcoming.
- The execution of a public duty is not sufficient consideration but going above and beyond an existing legal duty can be sufficient consideration.
- The performance of an existing contractual duty to a third party is consideration.
- The performance of an existing contractual duty to the promisor is not sufficient consideration, unless something extra is added.
- If the promisor has received some practical benefit from the agreement, this can be consideration for an existing contractual duty.
- The principle of practical benefit is not extended to part-payment of debt, and part-payment of debt is no consideration in satisfaction for the full debt, unless something extra is added, time/place of payment are changed, the sum/existence of the debt is in dispute, there is a composition agreement, or a third-party offers partial payment.
- Under certain circumstances where it would be unjust not do so, a contract without consideration can be enforced due to the equitable principle of promissory estoppel which can stop a party going back on their word.
- There needs to be a clear and unequivocal promise that the promisee relied on, promissory estoppel acts as a shield not as a sword, it suspends rights but does not extinguish them, and it should not be applied if the promisee has behaved unconscionable or inequitable.

Problem Question:

Sailing Sails sells boats. Ocean Farers organises sea holidays and charters out boats to holiday makers. Sailing Sails has a motorboat for sale that Ocean Farers is interested in buying. The two companies make a contract and as the boat is in quite a bad condition, they agree that Sailing Sails will first refurbish and paint the yacht. The contract gives a 6-week deadline for the work so that the boat will be ready for the summer holiday season.

Sailing Sails engages a small building company called Kwikbuild to refurbish the ship for £5,000. Kwikbuild agrees to get it done within 6 weeks. After 4 weeks Kwikbuild explains that it is more work than expected, and they ask Sailing Sails for an extra £2,000 so they can hire more staff. Sailing Sails is worried that the work will not be completed on time and agrees. In the final week Ocean Farers come by and check out the boat. They are happy with the progress and promise Kwikbuild £500 on completion.

The boat is finished within the six weeks but now Ocean Farers refuses to pay the £500 and Sailing Sails refuses to pay the extra £2,000.

Advise Kwikbuild

Sailing Sails and Kwikbuild have a contract for the refurbishment of the boat. There is executory consideration in the contract which has clear economic value and can thus be seen as sufficient. Kwikbuild gets £5,000 and Sailing Sails gets a refurbished boat.

When Kwikbuild asks for the extra £2,000 and Sailing Sails agrees there is no consideration. An existing contractual duty is not good consideration (***Stilk v Myrick [1809]***), however it might be possible to make a case that there is a practical benefit for Sailing Sails (***Williams v Roffey Bros & Nicholls (Contractors) Ltd [1990]***). If they cannot refurbish the ship on time Sailing Sails would be in breach of contract with Ocean Farers and they likely would have to pay damages so there is a clear benefit to the ship being refurbished on time. The caselaw surrounding practical benefit has no clearly established boundaries, although overall this approach is endorsed by the courts.

If the courts do not find a practical benefit, perhaps Kwikbuild could rely on promissory estoppel (***Central London Property v High Trees House [1947]***). It is important to remember that promissory estoppel is an equitable principle and available at the discretion of the court. Kwikbuild would have to prove that there was a clear and unequivocal promise by Sailing Sails, that they relied upon the promise made by Sailing Sails, that they have a pre-existing relationship with Sailing Sails, and that it would be unequitable for Sailing Sails to go back on their promise. However, promissory estoppel can only be used as a shield and not as a sword (***Combe v Combe [1951]***).

Ocean Farers promised Kwikbuild £500 upon completion, but did Kwikbuild offer any consideration in return? If there is no consideration, there would be no contract and it is a gratuitous promise. If consideration can be found, then this promise would be enforceable. A contractual duty owed to a third party can be sufficient consideration (***Scotson v Pegg [1861]***) and therefore completion of the boat for which Kwikbuild has a contract with Sailing Sails can serve as consideration for the £500 promise from Ocean Farers.

Key Cases

Central London Property v High Trees House [1947] KB 130: promissory estoppel
Chapell & Co Ltd v The Nestlé Co Ltd [1959] UKHL 1 & Bainbridge v Firmstone [1838] 8 A. & E. 743: sufficiency depends on circumstances
Collier v P&MJ Wright Holdings [2008] *EWCA Civ 1329:* Promissory estoppel can apply in cases of part-payment of debt
Collins v Godefroy [1831] *109 ER 1040:* performance of an existing legal duty
Combe v Combe [1951] *2 KB 215*: a promise not to sue should be asked
Cook v Wright [1861] *1 B & S 559*: giving up a worthless claim and a promise not to sue can be sufficient consideration
Cooper v Parker [1885] *15 CB 822*: genuine dispute about the existence or size of the debt
Coulls v Bagot's Executor and Trustee Ltd [1967] 119 CLR 460: joined promisee
Currie v Misa [1875] *LR 10 Ex 15*: classic definition of consideration
D&C Builders v Rees [1966] *2 WLR 28:* Promissory estoppel should not be used to help a party who has behaved in an unconscionable or inequitable way.
Dunlop Pneumatic Tyre Co. Ltd v Selfridge and Co. Ltd [1915] UKHL 1: modern definition of consideration
Eastwood v Kenyon [1840] *11 Ad&E 438*: past consideration is no consideration
Foakes v Beer [1884] *UKHL 1*: part-payment of debt is no consideration for the satisfaction of the full debt
Glasbrook Brothers v Glamorgan County Council [1925] *AC 270*: going above and beyond a legal duty can be sufficient consideration
Harris v Sheffield United Football Club [1988] 1 QB 77: act of the promisor causes the risk
Hartley v Ponsonby [1857] 7 EB 872: going above and beyond an existing contractual duty
Hirachand Punachand v Temple [1911] 2 KB 330: third party paying debt
Lampleigh v Brathwait [1615] *EWHC KB J17*: exception to the rule on past consideration
Pa On v Lau Yiu Long [1979] *UKPC 1*: past consideration is sufficient if the act is performed at the request of the promisor, if the parties understood that something would be expected in return for the act, and if the promise is enforceable as consideration if promised in advance.
Pinnel's Case [1602] *5 Co Rep 117*: changing time/place of payment or adding of trivial benefit constitutes sufficient consideration for part-payment of debt
Price v Easton [1833] *4 B&Ad 433:* promise can only be enforced if consideration provided
Re Selectmove Ltd [1995] *1 WLR 474*: practical benefit not extended to part payment of debt
Scotson v Pegg [1861] *6 H & N 295*: performance of an existing contractual duty to a third-party
Stilk v Myrick [1809] *170 ER 1168*: performance of an existing contractual duty
Thomas v Thomas [1842] *2 QB 851*: consideration should be sufficient but does not need to be adequate
Tweddle v Atkinson [1861] *121 ER 762*: consideration can move to a third party
Ward v Byham [1956] *All ER 318:* going above and beyond duty
Watkins & Sons Inc v Carrig 21 A.2d 591 (N.H. 1941): ending existing contract and making a new contract in case of contractual modifications
White v Bluett [1853] *LJ Ex 36*: example of when consideration is not sufficient
Williams v Roffey Bros & Nicholls (Contractors) Ltd [1990] *2 WLR 1153*: practical benefit can be sufficient consideration

CHAPTER V

RIGHTS OF THIRD PARTIES

Learning Outcomes:

After reading this chapter, you should be able to understand:

- ✓ What the doctrine of privity is;
- ✓ How the law sees the rights and obligations of third parties;
- ✓ How the Contract (Rights of Third Parties) Act 1999 changed the law;
- ✓ When third parties can enforce contractual rights.

Questions and Answers:

1. What do we mean with privity of contract?

Privity of contract is a common law doctrine and means that ***the contract only binds the parties to the contract.*** The contract cannot create any obligations for third parties. Traditionally in English common law, the contract also cannot create any rights for third parties. Even if the contract conferred a benefit on a third party, they could not sue to enforce this benefit. Under the Contracts (Rights of Third Parties) Act 1999 third parties can now enforce certain benefits conferred upon them by the contract.

2. What do we mean with *Ius Quasitum Tertio*?

This refers to the rights acquired by a third party under the contract. This third party is an ***intended beneficiary*** rather than an ***incidental beneficiary*** (*penitus extraneus*). The right of intended beneficiaries to sue upon the contract is not traditionally recognised under the common law but is accepted in other judicial systems, including under Scots law.

3. What do we mean by an intended beneficiary?

A contract could be beneficial for third parties without this being the intention of the contracting parties.

Example: If Rifka asks Albie to build a new fence for her garden, Rifka's neighbour Riley might benefit from having a nice new sturdy fence. Riley thus benefits from the contract between Rifka and Albie. However, it was never the intention of Rifka and Albie that Riley would benefit from the contract.

Sometimes the contract might be intended to benefit a group of people, but they would still not be intended beneficiaries.

Example: The university buys new computers for the library. Whilst the students will benefit from the computers, they would not be considered intended beneficiaries within the contractual relationship.

So, ***an intended beneficiary would be a person or group of persons who the contract clearly confers a benefit on.***

Example: Albie and Rifka make a contract to build a fence in Rifka's garden. Rifka puts into the contract that Albie should also build a new shed in Riley's garden. Riley is an intended beneficiary of the contract between Albie and Rifka.

4. What is the traditional common law position on third party rights?

The traditional position is that third parties cannot sue on the contract, even if the contract intents to confer a benefit upon them.

In Chapter IV Consideration & Promissory Estoppel we discussed the seminal case of ***Tweddle v Atkinson [1861]***. This case reflects the traditional common law position. When a young couple decided to get married the father of the groom and the father of the bride made a contract. They each promised to pay a sum of money to the groom after the wedding. The father of the bride died. The groom sued the estate of the father of the bride for the money. He could not recover the money because he was not a party to the contract.

Clearly, the groom was the intended beneficiary of the contract. The contract even specified he had the right to sue. However, as he was not a party to the contract (which was proven by the fact that he provided no consideration), he could not recover the money.

A drum containing chemicals was shipped from the United States to London. The contract between the carrier and the shipper contained a clause limiting liability in case of damages. The carrier engaged a group of stevedores under a separate contract. The stevedores damaged the drum and were sued for the full value of the drum. The stevedores wanted to rely on the limitation clause in the contract between the carrier and shipper. The court said that the stevedores could not rely on the clause because they were not part of the contract between the carrier and the shipper. It made no difference that they relied upon the term as a defence of action, rather than as a cause of action (***Scruttons Ltd v Midland Silicones Ltd [1962]***).

5. What is the key issue with the rule on privity?

The key problem is well-illustrated by the case of ***Dunlop Pneumatic Tyres v Selfridge [1915]***. ***Tweddle v Atkinson*** focused on whether consideration was provided to determine if the groom was part of the contract and therefore could sue, but ***Dunlop v Selfridge*** established more firmly the doctrine of privity independent from the issue of whether consideration had been provided.

Dunlop sold tyres to a company (Dew) which resold them. The contract stated that Dew was not allowed to sell the tyres below the list prices. They could however give a discount to any company that promised to observe the list prices. Dew sold tyres to Selfridge with the discount. Selfridge promised to observe the list prices. They did not. Dunlop decided to sue Selfridge. The court stated that Dunlop was not part of the contract between Selfridge and Dew. Selfridge made the promise not to sell below the list prices to Dew and had not made any promise to Dunlop.

Dew had not breached the contract with Dunlop. Dunlop therefore could not sue Dew. Dew had a contract with Selfridge and Selfridge had breached the contract. Dew could sue Selfridge. The main issue was that Dew had suffered no loss. The breach of contract did not affect them. Dew had no reason to sue Selfridge. It would just be an inconvenience for them. And even if they sued Selfridge, it would be difficult for them to get any compensation. After all, Dew had suffered no loss. So, what damages could they get apart from nominal damages? The only company that had suffered a loss was Dunlop who now faced unfair competition.

The problem is thus that ***the party that can sue upon the contract has suffered no loss***, and ***the party that suffered a loss cannot sue upon the contract***.

In ***Tweddle v Atkinson*** the father of the groom could have sued the estate of the father of the bride for breach of contract. However, the father of the groom had suffered no actual loss as the money was intended for the groom.

6. Is it possible to sue on the contract if you have suffered no loss?

In principle, you can only recover damages for an actual loss you have suffered yourself. If a third party who was a beneficiary under the contract has suffered a loss & the party to the contract has not been affected and has suffered no loss, ***the contracting party can sue for breach of contract but would not be able to recover losses on behalf of the third party***. They would only be able to recover their own losses, and in the absence of these can only get nominal damages. However, there are some exceptions.

It is sometimes possible to ***recover damages for yourself and the other beneficiaries of the contract.*** In ***Jackson v Horizon Holidays [1975]***, Mr Jackson had arranged a holiday for himself and his family. The holiday did not meet the expectations of the contract. The court held that Mr Jackson could recover the loss for himself and his entire family (even if the family was not part of the contract) because it was clear that the contract had been concluded so that the whole family would enjoy a nice holiday. Whilst the family could not enforce the contract, Mr Jackson could enforce it on behalf of his family and himself.

The court made this decision in light of the earlier case of ***Lloyds v Harper [1880]*** whereby Lloyds sued the guarantor of an underwriter who had defaulted on some issued policies. Whilst Lloyds had suffered no direct loss the court allowed Lloyds to recover the full amount that was due to the policy holders. Lush LJ: *"I consider it to be an established rule of law that where a contract is made with A for the benefit of B, A can sue on the contract for the benefit of B and can recover all that B could have recovered if the contract had been made with B himself."*

In ***Woodar Investment Dev Ltd v Wimpey Construction UK Ltd [1980]*** the court stated that the passage from ***Lloyds v Harper*** should be confined to situations where there is an agent with the authority to sue on behalf of the principal. The House of Lords made it clear that ***Jackson*** does not represent the general rule.

There are also some limited exceptions to ***reflect transferred loss in relation to contracts transferring property rights*** (***Linden Gardens Trust v Lenesta Sludge Disposals [1994]***).

7. How could a third party sue upon the contract before the Contracts (Rights of Third Parties) Act 1999 was enacted?

The third party would need to prove that they were part of the contract and had provided consideration.

In ***Beswick v Beswick [1967]***, Peter Beswick entered into a contract to sell his coal business to his nephew John. Part of the agreement was that John would employ Peter for the rest of his life and that he would pay £5 a week to Ruth, Peter's wife. Peter died and John stopped paying the £5. Ruth sued John. Ruth was not part of the contract between John and Peter and had provided no consideration in her personal capacity as beneficiary. However, as she was also the administrator of Peter's estate the court reasoned that she had become part of the contract through her role as administrator. The issue was that the estate had not suffered any loss from the lack of payment, whereas Mrs Beswick personally had suffered a loss. The House of Lords decided to enforce the payment as specific performance, given that it would be difficult to ascertain the loss the estate had suffered (if any).

8. What exceptions are there to the rule?

- Collateral contracts
- Trust of a contractual right
- Assignment
- Agency
- Negotiable instruments
- Tort
- Statutory exceptions (including the Contracts (Rights of Third Parties) Act 1999)

***Collateral contracts*:** This refers to side contracts which rely for their existence upon the main contract. The side contract is the consideration for entering into the main contract.

Trust of a contractual right: A trust refers to a relationship whereby one party transfers property to another party who then holds the property for the benefit of a third party. There is no contract with the beneficiary. However, under a trust the beneficiary has the right to enforce the contract in equity.

A charter party contained a clause for the benefit of the charterers' brokers: "*A commission of three per cent on the estimated gross amount of hire is due to Leopold Walford (London), Ltd, on signing this charter (ship lost or not lost).*" The court reasoned that the brokers nominated the charterers to contract on their behalf and that therefore the charterers could sue under the agreement as trustees of the brokers (***Les Affreteurs Réunis Société Anonyme v Leopold Walford (London) Ltd [1919]***). The parties must have had the intention to create a trust (***Re Schebsman [1944]***).

Agency contracts: In ***Dunlop Pneumatic Tyres v Selfridge*** Viscount Haldane said that if an agent entered into a contract on behalf of the principal, the principal could sue under the contract even if he was not named in the contract.

Negotiable instruments: Instruments that contain a guarantee to pay a specific amount of money to the person in possession of the instrument. An example is a cheque. The person who draws the cheque provides instructions to the bank to pay a third party a sum of money. The third party acquires rights even if he is not part of the contract.

Tort: A third party can sue if they have suffered a loss as a result of negligence resulting from the contractual obligation between the defendant and another party. In ***Donoghue v Stevenson [1932]*** the claimant became ill after drinking ginger beer with a decomposing snail in it. Her friend had bought the beer for her; therefore, the claimant was not part of the sale contract. The House of Lords held the defendant liable to the claimant in tort.

Statutory exceptions include:

Section 11 of the Married Women's Property Act 1882: Life Assurance policy for the benefit of a wife, husband and/or children shall create a trust in favour of these persons and any moneys payable thereunder shall not form part of the insured's estate or be subject to his debts.

Section 14(2) of the Marine Insurance Act 1906: Insurance on one's behalf and for the benefit of other interested persons.

Section 148(7) of the Road Traffic Act 1988: The insurance policy issuer is liable to indemnify the persons specified in the policy in respect of any liability covered thereunder.

Section 2 of the Carriage of Goods by Sea Act 1992: The lawful holder of the bill of lading is entitled to sue under the contract of carriage as if he was part of that contract.

9. How has the law changed with the Contract (Rights of Third Parties) Act 1999?

Under the Act ***third parties can enforce certain rights conferred upon them by the contract. It does not abolish the doctrine of privity***. It also does not affect the existing exceptions discussed above. It applies to contracts concluded on or after 11 May 2000.

Section 1(1) confers upon a person who is not a party to the contract the right to enforce a term of the contract if:

a) The contract expressly provides that he may, or
b) The term purports to confer a benefit on him

Section 1(2) states that subsection (1)(b) does not apply if on proper construction of the contract it appears that the parties did not intend the term to be enforceable by a third party.

The Act creates a rebuttable presumption. Evidence is needed to prove that no right was intended to be bestowed upon a third party.

The parties can include ***a clause in the contract which excludes the right of a third party to sue upon the contract.***

Section 1(3) discusses the identity of the third party. The third-party must be expressly identified either by name, as a member of a class, or as answering a particular description, but need not be in existence when the contract is concluded.

The latter includes an unborn child, a future spouse, a company that will be incorporated in the future, a partner who will join a partnership later on...

The person does not have to be named, but we need to be able to identify them. For instance, if Rifka and Albie make a contract whereby Albie promises to build a shed for Riley then Riley is identified by name. Rifka and Albie could also make a contract where Albie promises to build a shed for Rifka's neighbour to the right. That does not identify Riley by name, but as she is Rifka's neighbour to the right she has been identified as a third-party beneficiary.

The third party does not need to know about the contract (***Charity Commission v Franjee [2014]***).

Section 1(4) states that third party's right is subject to and must be in accordance with any other relevant terms of the contract.

Section 1(5) states that any remedies available to a contractual party are also available to the third party in the event of a breach of contract.

Section 1(6) states that the third party may enforce or avail himself on an exclusion or limitation clause in the contract

Section 2 of the Act discusses variation and rescission of the contract:

> (1) Consent of third party (who has the right to enforce) is required before the contract can be rescinded or varied if—
>
> (a)the third party has communicated his assent to the term to the promisor,
>
> (b)the promisor is aware that the third party has relied on the term, or
>
> (c)the promisor can reasonably be expected to have foreseen that the third party would rely on the term and the third party has in fact relied on it.
>
> (2) Assent may be by words or conduct, and (b) must be received by the promisor.

Example: if Rifka and Albie make a contract and under that contract Albie has to construct a shed for Riley and Riley does not know about this and has not made any preparations in reliance on that promise then Rifka and Albie can vary their agreement without Riley's consent. However, if Riley is aware of the promise, has said that she agrees with Albie building her a shed, and has already started to prepare the garden for the construction then Rifka and Albie will need Riley's consent before they can vary the contract.

The contract is still enforceable by the promisee (*Section 4*) and any award to a third party is to be reduced to such an extent as the court thinks appropriate to take account of the sum recovered by the promisee *(Section 5. Protection of Promisor from Double Liability*).

Example: Diego and Tamera enter into a contract. Under the contract Tamera will get £3,000 and Diego will get a car. However, the car is intended not for Diego but for Diego's friend Dorian. The contract names Dorian as beneficiary. Diego rents a parking space where Dorian can park the car and pays for a parking permit. Diego gives the money to Tamera, but Tamera breaches the contract and does not deliver the car. Now, both Dorian and Diego can sue on the contract. Tamera could be liable to both. For instance, Diego has spent money to rent a parking space and get the permit in reliance on the contract. Dorian has not received the car and must now rent a car until he buys a new one. They have therefore both suffered a loss. The court will take into account the damages that Tamera owes to Diego when deciding how much she owes to Dorian.

Section 7 deals with the issue of exemption clauses: Third parties cannot challenge the fairness or reasonableness of a term of the contract.

10. What are the exceptions to the Act?

These are discussed in Section 6:

- A contract on a bill of exchange, promissory note or another negotiable instrument;
- A contract binding on a company and its members under section 33 of the Companies Act 2006 (effect of the company's constitution);
- Agreement involving a limited liability partnership and its members;
- Any term of a contract of employment against an employee;
- Any term of a worker's contract against a worker (including a home worker), or;
- Any term of a relevant contract against an agency worker;
- A contract for the carriage of goods by sea, or;

- A contract for the carriage of goods by rail or road, or for the carriage of cargo by air, subject to the rules of the appropriate international transport convention.

11. Why was the law changed?

If the parties clearly intended to confer a benefit to a third party, then not allowing the third party to enforce that benefit goes counter to ***the intentions of the parties***. This again shows how the intentions of the contracting parties are leading and how the law is moving towards recognising the primacy of these intentions which can also be seen by how the courts have qualified the doctrine of certainty (See Chapter III) and consideration (See Chapter IV).

The common law position also created ***injustice for third parties*** (think for instance of Dunlop, which suffered a loss because of the actions of Selfridge but could not recover its losses). The third party is dependent upon the promisee to sue but the promisee may not want to because they suffered no loss. Furthermore, even if they did sue, they likely would not be able to recover the loss that the third party has suffered.

In other jurisdictions, including most EU Member States and Scotland, there is no such far-reaching privity doctrine and therefore third parties could always enforce their rights under the contract. Changing the law means that English contract law is now more compatible with transnational commercial law.

12. Can a contract impose obligations on a third party?

No, the contract cannot impose any obligations on a third party.

Example: Albie and Rifka make a contract to refurbish Rifka's garden. In the contract they put a clause to state that Albie can access Riley's garden so he can carry out the work more easily. Riley is not part of this contract and therefore Albie and Rifka cannot put this obligation on her. Riley is not contractually obliged to allow Albie access to her garden.

Summary:

- Under the common law doctrine of privity, a third party cannot enforce a contract, even if he is a beneficiary to the contract. There are some exceptions to this rule.
- With the enactment of the Contract (Rights of Third Parties) Act 1999 it possible for a third party to enforce their rights under the contract.
- The third party should be identified in the contract, the contract should either expressly provide that they can sue, or the contract should confer a benefit on the third party. This does not apply if upon proper

construction of the contract it appears that the parties did not intend the right to be enforceable by a third party.

- A contract cannot confer any obligations on a third party.

Problem Question:

Rahiya and Bart have made a contract for the sale of several of Rahiya's possessions including a computer, some furniture, and a car in return for £10,000. The contract also includes a reference to Bart's friend Raoul who is promised in the contract that he will receive the car.

1) Can Raoul sue upon the contract if Rahiya does not include the car in the sale?

Traditionally, under the common law only the parties to the contract can sue on the contract. Raoul is the beneficiary of the clause, but he has provided no consideration for that promise. Therefore, he is not a party to the contract. Bart is a party to the contract and can therefore sue on the contract. However, Bart might not want to because he was never going to receive the car anyway and he does not care that Rahiya breached the contract. Bart could also decide to sue but as he cannot prove he suffered an actual loss (as the car was not for him) it would be difficult to get more than nominal damages. Of course, if Bart can prove that he did suffer a loss it would be different, and he could be compensated for his actual loss.

This has changed with the Contract (Rights of Third Parties) Act 1999. Raoul can now sue Rahiya even though he is not part of the contract.

For that to happen either the contract must state that Raoul can sue (Section 1(1)(a)) or the contract confers a benefit upon him (Section 1(1)(b)) such as giving Raoul the car. If Rahiya can prove that the parties did not intend for Raoul to be able to sue upon the contract, then Raoul cannot do so (Section 1(2)). Raoul should also be identifiable as a third party, either because he is named or because he is described (Section 1(3)). Given that the contract contains a reference to Raoul it is likely that he will satisfy this criterion.

2) Can Rahiya and Bart vary or end the contract, so that Raoul will no longer be getting the car?

Under Section 2 of the Contract (Rights of Third Parties) Act 1999 Rahiya and Bart can vary or end their agreement without Raoul's consent unless:

a) Raoul has agreed to receive the car
b) Raoul has started to rely upon the term, for instance by renting a garage or selling his old car

c) It was foreseeable that Raoul would rely upon the promise, for instance because he already discussed with Rahiya and Bart that he would sell his old car.

Key Cases

Tweddle v Atkinson [1861] *EWHC J57:* if a third party has provided no consideration they cannot sue upon the contract even if they are an intended beneficiary

Dunlop Pneumatic Tyres v Selfridge [1915] *AC 847:* only the parties to the contract can sue. Exceptions for trusts and principal/agent contracts.

Jackson v Horizon Holidays [1975] *1 WLR 1468:* if the contract was made for the benefit on an entire group, the party can sue upon his own behalf as well as that of the others

Woodar Investment Dev Ltd v Wimpey Construction UK Ltd [1980] *1 WLR 277:* only in principal-agent situations should it be possible to recover loss for a third party.

Lloyds v Harper [1880] *16 Ch. D. 290:* recovering loss for a third party

Beswick v Beswick [1967] *UKHL 2:* specific performance if party has suffered no loss

Re Schebsman [1944] *Ch 83*: parties must have intended to create a trust

Donoghue v Stevenson [1932] UKHL 100: negligence under tort

CHAPTER VI

CAPACITY

Learning Outcomes:

After reading this chapter, you should be able to understand:

- ✓ The capacity of natural persons to enter into contracts;
- ✓ Under which circumstances minors can enter into a contract;
- ✓ The capacity of mentally incapacitated people to enter into contracts;
- ✓ The capacity of companies to contract.

Questions and Answers:

1. What do we mean with capacity to contract?

Having capacity to contract refers to having the ***legal capacity*** to contract. In principle the law assumes natural persons and legal persons (such as companies) have capacity. The law takes a wide view of capacity and only two categories of natural persons do not (always) have legal capacity: ***Minors and people that are mentally incapacitated***; including people that are temporarily incapacitated such as drunk people.

2. What is the position of the law on minors?

The position of minors is governed by the Minors' Contract Act 1987. The general rule is that ***minors are not bound by the contracts they conclude***.

There are some exceptions:

- Contracts for necessaries;
- Beneficiary contracts for employment and education;
- Contracts that continue past the attainment of majority and are not repudiated
- (voidable contracts).

Minors are individuals below the age of 18 (this was changed from 21 to 19 through the Family Law Reform Act 1969).

3. What are contracts for necessaries?

Necessaries includes ***goods and services that are necessary in daily life***. The Sale of Goods Act 1979 defines these in Section 3(2): *"'necessaries' means goods* *suitable to the condition in life of the minor or other person concerned and to his actual requirements at the time of sale and delivery."* This includes items necessary for survival such as food, shelter, and clothes.

These contracts are binding on the minor. To establish whether the items are necessaries there are two tests:

1) Do these goods/services fit the condition of life of the minor?
2) Are the goods/services actually necessary at time of sale?

Alderson J stated in ***Chappel v Cooper [1844]***: *"The subject-matter and extent of the contract may vary according to the state and condition of the infant himself. His clothes may be fine or coarse according to his rank; his education may vary according to the station he is to fill.... the things furnished are essential to the existence and reasonable advantage and comfort of the infant contractor"* (in older cases minors are usually referred to as infants in line with the now repealed Infant Relief Act 1874).

In ***Peters v Fleming [1840]*** a student contracted for jewellery (rings, pins, and a watch chain). The student later refused to honour the contract and said that he was not bound as he was a minor. The court held that the jewellery could be seen as necessaries for the student because of his background as his family had money and his father was an MP. So, the jewellery was seen as being necessary given the condition of life that the student was used to.

In ***Nash v Inman [1840]*** a Cambridge student, son of a wealthy architect, contracted with a tailor for eleven waistcoats. The student refused to pay, and his father also refused to pay stating that the son had quite enough clothes and did not need more. The court held that the contract did not satisfy both tests for establishing whether these were necessaries. Whilst the clothes were suitable for the condition of life of the student, they were not necessary to his actual requirements at the time of sale and delivery.

If it is satisfied that the contract is for necessaries, the minor is liable to pay a ***reasonable price*** for these (Section 3(2) of Sale of Goods Act 1979). A reasonable price is not necessarily the same as the price agreed in the contract.

Minors are not bound by onerous contractual terms. In ***Fawcett v Smethurst [1914]*** a minor hired a car. The car hire was seen as necessary. The contract contained a clause under which the minor would be liable for any damage to the vehicle, regardless of how it was caused. The court held that the clause was onerous, and the minor was not bound by this.

4. What is a beneficial contract of service?

These include contracts of employment, education, and apprenticeship. This has been extended to include other type of professional contracts such as publishing contracts (***Chaplin v Leslie Frewin (Publishers) Ltd [1966]***). As long as these contracts are substantially beneficial for the minor they will be binding on the minor. Even if some of the terms are onerous the contract can still be enforced if it is overall beneficial for the minor.

In ***Clements v London and North Western Railway [1894]*** a minor entered into a contract for employment with the railway. He joined the company's insurance scheme. This meant he would give up his right to sue for personal injury under the Employers Liability Act 1880. The Court held that whilst this term was indeed onerous, the insurance was more beneficial to the minor because it offered more extensive coverage than the Act did. The contract was therefore held to be beneficial for the minor.

The rule that the contract can be binding on the minor if it is beneficial to him/her is confined to contracts of employment, apprenticeship, education, and similar. It does not apply to other contracts such as sale contracts (See for instance ***Cowern v Nield [1812]***).

If the terms are not beneficial for the minor, then he/she is not bound by the contract. A 14-year-old girl concluded a contract for an apprenticeship for stage dancing. The contract stated that the girl could not marry until after seven years, she required consent of the employer to take up other professional employment, would be paid less than was usual, and was not even guaranteed work. The court concluded that the contract was not for her benefit, as the terms were onerous and clearly benefited the employer more than they benefitted her (***De Francesco v Barnum [1890]***).

This can be contrasted with ***Doyle v White City Stadium [1935]*** where an underage boxer did not want to be held to a contract that stated that he would lose his fees if he was disqualified. The court held that the overall contract was for his benefit and would aid him in his career.

5. Which contracts are voidable for the minor?

This is confined to ***continuing contracts whereby the minor acquires something of a permanent nature***, such as shares or a partnership. These contracts are binding on the minor if he does not repudiate them before attaining the age of majority or within a reasonable time thereafter (***Edwards v Carter [1893]***).

If the minor repudiates the contract, he can under some circumstances recover any money he paid if there is a total failure of consideration (***Cope v Overton [1833]***), but not if he has received consideration (***Spielberg v Scala (Leeds) Ltd [1923]***).

Trading contracts the minor concluded can be ratified by the minor upon reaching majority.

6. Are there any remedies available against minors?

If someone enters into a contract with a minor and they breach the contract, there are some remedies available:

- Remedies in tort
- Restitution
- Guarantees

Remedies in tort: A minor may be liable for the commission of a tort, but this liability cannot be used as a way to enforce a contract on the minor. In ***Leslie Ltd v Sheill [1914]*** a moneylender sued a minor who lied about his age so he could borrow money. The court held if they allowed the moneylender to succeed his claim in tort then this would be an indirect way of enforcing the contract.

This can be contrasted with ***Burnard v Haggis [1863]*** where a minor concluded a contract for hiring a horse. The contract contained a provision that he would not be allowed to jump with the horse. He did so anyway, and the horse was injured. The minor was held liable for the injuries of the horse.

Restitution: Available as an equitable remedy if the minor has obtained certain goods fraudulently. The minor could be made to return the goods. However, if the goods are already consumed or altered in such a way that they cannot be returned, the minor will not be liable to pay for them instead.

Section 3 Minors' Contracts Act 1987:

> *The court may, if it is just and equitable to do so, require the defendant to transfer to the plaintiff any property acquired by the defendant under the contract, or any property representing it.*

Guarantees: If a contract with a minor is guaranteed by a guarantor, the contract can possible be enforced against this guarantor.

Section 2 Minors' Contracts Act 1987

> *Where—*

(a)a guarantee is given in respect of an obligation of a party to a contract made after the commencement of this Act, and

(b)the obligation is unenforceable against him (or he repudiates the contract) because he was a minor when the contract was made, the guarantee shall not for that reason alone be unenforceable against the guarantor.

7. What about contracts with people that are mentally incapacitated?

This would include people that are drunk and unable to understand what they agreed to do because of a high level of intoxication.

These contracts are ***valid except if the individual is incapable of understanding the nature of the transaction and the other contracting party is aware of this.*** The aim is to prevent people from taking advantage of others who are not in a position to understand what they are agreeing to.

If the other contracting party is not aware of the condition of the mentally incapacitated person, the contract will usually be valid (***Hart v O'Connor [1985]***).

This is thus different from the law on contracting with minors. Even if the other contracting party is not aware that the person that they are contracting with is underage, the contract would not be valid, unless the contract falls under the exceptions discussed above. In the case of mentally incapacitated people, it is up to the person making the claim to prove that the other party was aware of his incapacity.

The necessaries exception applies for mentally incapacitated persons, and the person must pay a reasonable price for these necessaries (Section 3(2) Sale of Goods Act 1979 and Section (7)1 Mental Capacity Act 2005). Note that this says reasonable price, which is not necessarily the same as the full price agreed under the contract. The law usually does not interfere in the price of goods so if someone wants to sell something for a price way beyond its actual value and someone else is willing to buy for that price the contract would be valid. However, in capacity cases the law can interfere and stipulate a reasonable price that should be paid.

A person who is certified as being insane cannot freely dispose of their property because their property belongs to the court, therefore any contract entered into which involves disposing of property would be void (Part VIII of the Mental Health Act 1983).

8. What about corporations?

Before the enactment of the Companies Act 2006 a company could not contract for anything that was considered *ultra vires.* Companies have a Memorandum and Articles of Association. These list the purpose and the objects of the company. Any contract outside of these objects was considered *ultra vires* and therefore void.

Example: Pinetree Exports has the object to export timber around the world. Any contract it makes in relation to that object is acceptable. This would include of course contracts for the sale of timber, but also contracts that are necessary to support its business such as a contract for new computers. However, if Pinetree Exports suddenly started contracting for buying and selling ice cream this would have been considered *ultra vires.*

This changed with the Companies Act 2006 (Section 39(A) and Section 40). ***Contracts that the company enters into are now enforceable regardless of anything in the company's constitution.*** This ensures certainty for contracting parties who can now be sure that the contract will be valid.

Ultra Vires still applies in the relationship between the shareholders and the company.

Statutory Corporations created by Acts of Parliament for specific purposes: The creating statute specifies the purposes for which the corporation can contract and any contracts outside of this are *ultra vires* and therefore void.

Chartered Corporations are set up by Royal Charter: If they enter into contracts contrary to the spirits of the Charter, the Charter can be revoked

Limited Liability Partnerships (LLP): Section 1(3) of the Liability Partnership Act 2000 states that the LLP has unlimited capacity to contract

Summary:

- Contracts with minors are generally unenforceable, unless these are contracts for necessaries, beneficial contracts of service, or voidable contracts not repudiated before or within a reasonable time after attaining majority.
- Contracts with drunks and mentally incapacitated people are voidable if the person did not understand the nature of the transaction and the other person knows of this.
- After the enactment of the Companies Act 2006, companies now have unlimited capacity to contract with third parties.

Problem Question:

Jay (15) and Mark (17) form a very successful local band. Drew, a band manager hears them play and wants to help them build their career and get a record deal for them. He convinces the boys to sign a contract. Jay signs a contract that says Drew has exclusive distribution rights for all his music, will get 30% of Jay's earnings and Jay is not allowed to take on any other employment without Drew's permission. Mark does not want to sign that contract and proposes they enter into a partnership instead under which they will together market the band and share earnings 75% for Mark and 25% for Drew. Drew agrees. The boys are quite successful and are soon playing gigs every night around the country and make their first record. After speaking with others in the industry they realise the contracts they have with Drew are not very good and they want out. By now Jay is 17 and Mark is 19.

What advice would you give Jay and Mark?

Jay is still a minor. However, a contract for necessaries or a beneficiary service contract could be valid (*Minors' Contract Act 1987*). An employment contract falls under a beneficiary service contract. It seems that Drew's management is successful because he has the boys playing more concerts and also managed to get the boys a record deal. Therefore, the contract is beneficiary for Jay. However, the terms of the contract could be seen as particularly onerous, and this could mean that the contract is not binding on Jay (***De Francesco v Barnum [1890]***). It depends on whether the court finds that the contract as a whole is beneficiary for Jay and not too lopsided in favour of Drew (***Clements v London and North Western Railway [1894]***).

Mark has formed a partnership with Drew and has now attained the age of majority. This is considered a voidable contract and should be repudiated before reaching majority or within a reasonable time after (***Edwards v Carter [1893]***). It could be that because Mark is now 19 this reasonable time has passed, and he can no longer repudiate the contract. He could perhaps terminate the partnership on other grounds, but it could be that he can no longer rely on being a minor when he entered into the contract. If the court does decide that he has repudiated within a reasonable time of reaching majority then he can only recuperate monies under it if he has received no consideration in return (***Spielberg v Scala (Leeds) Ltd [1923]***). This is likely not the case as he has received consideration in the form of increased concerts, a record deal, and other career benefits.

Key Cases

Chappel v Cooper [1844] *13 M & W 252*: what falls under necessaries for minors
Peters v Fleming [1840] *151 ER 314*: condition in life influences what are necessaries
Nash v Inman [1840] 2 KB 1: even when the contract is for necessaries that fit the condition of life of the minor, they also have to be necessary at the time of sale and delivery
Fawcett v Smethurst [1914] *84 LJKB 473*: onerous contracts are not binding on the minor
Clements v London and North Western Railway [1894] *2 Q.B.49*: even if some terms are onerous, as long as the contract is substantially beneficial for the minor, the contract is valid
Cowern v Nield [1812] *2 K.B. 419*: a beneficiary contract on the minor is restricted to employment, education, and apprenticeship contracts.
De Francesco v Barnum [1890] *45 Ch D 430:* If the terms of the contract are such that they do not benefit the minor, the minor is not bound by the contract.
Edwards v Carter [1893] *AC 360:* repudiation within a reasonable time after attaining majority
Spielberg v Scala (Leeds) Ltd [1923]*:* minor cannot recuperate money from a repudiated contract if he has received consideration in return
Leslie Ltd v Sheill [1914] *3 K.B.607*: action in tort cannot be used as an indirect way to enforce a void contract
Hart v O'Connor [1985] *UKPC 1:* awareness of lack of mental capacity

CHAPTER VII

TERMS OF THE CONTRACT

Learning Outcomes:

After reading this chapter, you should be able to understand:

- ✓ The difference between terms and representations;
- ✓ How the parol evidence rule works;
- ✓ What implied and express terms are;
- ✓ How terms become part of the contract.

Questions and Answers:

1. How do we define the terms of the contract?

The terms of the contract define the rights and obligations of the parties to the contract. They are also called contract clauses. You will also often hear the wording 'terms and conditions.' The focus is on what the parties have substantively agreed on their rights and obligations under the contract. The parties are free to decide what they want to include in the terms of the contract, they are only limited by the boundaries of the law.

In written contracts it is easy to know what the terms are because they are written down. However, in oral and mixed contracts it can be much more difficult to decide what the terms are because the parties might have a different recollection of what was agreed, or they never talked about certain issues.

If there is a dispute between the parties the court will first refer to the contract, and only if the parties have not made any provisions for the specific issue on which there is a dispute will the court ***use the law to fill in the gaps in the contract.***

2. What is the difference between terms and representations?

Representations are not part of the contract. They are statements made to induce a party to enter into a contract, but they are not part of the contract. Especially in oral contracts it can be difficult to decide whether a statement is a term or a representation.

Terms are part of the contract. The breach of a term allows the innocent party to bring action for a breach of contract (See Chapter XIII). The breach of a representation allows to bring action for a misrepresentation (See Chapter X). The remedies available for misrepresentation differ from those for a breach of contracts.

To distinguish between a term and a representation the court looks at ***the objective intentions of the parties.*** The court takes into account all evidence and will decide based on the available facts (***Heilbut, Symons & Co v Buckleton [1913]***).

If a statement is made is made by ***a person with expert skill and knowledge*** on the subject matter, it is more likely that the statement will be held to be a term of the contract (***Oscar Chess Ltd v Williams [1957]***). If the person does not have any expertise or skill, it is more likely to be held to be a representation (***Dick Bentley Productions Ltd v Harold Smith (Motors) Ltd [1965]***). ***A collateral warranty*** is an implied promise that a specific statement was made with reasonable skill and care (***Esso Petroleum Ltd v Maddon [1976]***).

The more important the statement is, the more likely it will be held to be a term. In ***Bannerman v White [1861]***, the buyer of hops told the seller that he would not even bother to ask for the price if the hops had been treated with sulphur. The seller confirmed that the hops had not been sulphur-treated and they concluded a contract. When the buyer found out some of the hops had been treated with sulphur he refused to pay and was sued by the seller who claimed the statement was not a term of the contract. The court held that the buyer had made very clear that the lack of sulphur treatment was very important for him and therefore the statement was considered a term of the contract.

The timing of the statement is also important. The more time that passes between making the statement and the conclusion of the contract, the less likely that the statement will be regarded as a contractual term.

Strong statements are much more likely to be considered terms of the contract. For instance, if the seller expresses in very strong words that the object has certain properties or reassures the buyer of the quality. See for instance ***Schawel v Reade [1913]***, where the seller of a horse said: *'you need not look for anything: The horse is perfectly sound'* and contrast this with ***Ecay v Godfrey [1947]*** where the seller of a boat stated that the boat was sound, but that it would be a good idea for the buyer to have the boat surveyed anyway. In the first instance the statement was held to be a term whereas in the second instance the statement was a representation because the seller already expressed certain reservations as to the state of the boat.

Terms should also be distinguished from ***'mere puff'*** which include advertisement like statements such as 'you will never find a washing powder that gets more stains out.'

3. What is the parol evidence rule?

Oftentimes, the parties will first discuss the terms on which they wish to contract. During such negotiations many different statements will be made. In those negotiations the parties often conclude an oral contract and subsequently reduce the oral contract into writing.

Where the parties ***reduce an oral contract into writing***, generally what is written will be regarded as the terms of the contract. Any statements that were made during the negotiations, but not included in the written contract are generally regarded as a representation. The idea is that if a statement was important enough to be a term of the contract, then the parties would have included this statement in the written contract (***Henderson v Arthur [1907]***).

The ***parol evidence rule*** means that if there is a written contract and the intention of the parties was that the written contract would contain all the express terms of the contract, any other evidence to change, contradict, add to, or subtract from the contract will be inadmissible. This other evidence does not just include any oral statements, but also emails, text messages, notes, and other written documents.

The parol evidence rule is a ***presumption*** and can be rebutted (***Gillespie Bros v Cheney, Eggar & Co [1896]***).

Example: Simon sells his car to Cara. They discuss the different aspects of the sale which includes the delivery date. They settle on 5 March. The written contract is signed on 4 March and does not include that date but says that delivery should be within 3 weeks after concluding the contract, unless the parties have made different arrangements when concluding the contract. The parol evidence rule would suggest that the car does not need to be delivered on 5 March but can be delivered to Cara any time before 25 March. However, the rule is a presumption and therefore can be rebutted. The contract makes clear that if a different arrangement is made this arrangement is part of the contract. This could rebut the rule and the car would still need to be delivered to Cara on 5 March.

In principle the parties can make ***oral variations to written contracts***. However, if a written contract contains a clause prohibiting oral variation, any variation of the contract should be in writing (***Rock Advertising Ltd v MWB Business Exchange Centres Ltd [2018]***).

There are many exceptions to the parol evidence rule:

- *Rectifications* (Evidence that shows that the written agreement did not accurately record the oral agreement).
- *Partially written agreements* (There is a written agreement, but the parties clearly intended it to be qualified by other statements not contained in the written agreement. See for instance the above example of Simon and Cara).
- *Operation of the contract* (Extrinsic evidence is admissible to show that the operation of the written contract depends on some event or condition (*Pym v Campbell [1856]*).
- *Custom and usage* (Evidence is admissible to show that a term should be qualified by a custom or trade usage. In *Smith v Wilson [1832]*, it was shown that under trade custom 1,000 rabbits as written in the contract, actually meant 1,200 rabbits).
- *Course of dealing* (If the parties have regularly done business before, course of dealing contrary to the written contract can be admissible in court).

Another exemption is the ***collateral contract***. This is an oral statement which is treated as a contractual promise and becomes an (oral) side contract to the main (written) contract. In ***J. Evans & Son (Portsmouth) v Andrea Merzario Ltd [1976]*** a contract was concluded for the shipping of some machinery. The claimant wanted the machinery to be stored below deck so it would not rust. The defendant assured the claimant that this would be done. However, the machinery was transported on deck in the end and fell overboard. The oral assurance was not in the written contract, but the court stated that it could be enforced regardless because without this promise the main contract would not have come into existence.

If the parties want to ensure that no oral statement or other evidence is part of the contract, they can introduce an ***entire agreement clause*** in the contract.

4. What is the difference between express and implied terms of the contract?

Express terms are those terms which the parties have explicitly agreed on.

Implied terms are those terms which the parties have not explicitly agreed on, but which are nevertheless part of the contract.

Terms can be implied by:

- Statute
- Usage and custom
- By the court in fact or in law

5. What are terms implied by statute?

Terms implied by statute are those terms that are part of the contract because statutory law states that they are.

An example is the Sale of Goods Act 1979 which implies among others the following terms in a sales contract:

Section 12:

- That the seller has the right to sell the goods at the time property passes.
- That the goods are free from any charge or encumbrance not known to the buyer.

Section 13:

- That if the goods are sold by description, then the goods will correspond to that description.

Section 14:

- That the goods are of satisfactory quality.

There is no need for the parties to include these terms into their sales contract. The terms are already part of the contract.

Example: Samson, who runs a wholesale business, sells his bike to Giovanni, who owns a bike shop. They agree on a price and date. They write this down on a piece of paper. After the bike is sold Giovanni discovers that the brakes do not work. Giovanni complains to Samson who says that he never told Giovanni the brakes were working. Whilst indeed this was not an express term of the contract, it is implied by statute as the bike should be of satisfactory quality. So, unless Giovanni and Samson excluded this deliberately from their contract, the quality requirement is part of the contract.

If Samson made clear to Giovanni the brakes were not working and Giovanni agreed to buy the bike anyway, the express terms of their contract would trump the terms implied by statute (unless these are mandatory laws).

6. What are terms implied from usage or custom?

In different trades and localities, merchants have developed customs and trade usages. These are especially common in commodity trades. If they are not expressly and precisely excluded from the contract, they are considered implied contractual terms.

The parties should know the custom or usage or ought to have known of its existence. If the custom/usage is widespread, pleading ignorance of its existence is not an accepted excuse.

Custom and (trade) usage are often used interchangeably, but they are not the same. Custom has a higher threshold and depends upon the parties believing that they were legally bound to follow the custom. Custom must be 'notorious, certain, and reasonable' (***Cunliffe-Owen v Teather & Greenwood [1967]***). For trade usages there is no need to prove that the parties believe that the usage is legally binding. The court decides on observance whether a certain practice should be considered a trade usage.

7. How are terms implied by the court?

These can be ***implied by fact.*** Those terms are not stated in the contract, but they are necessary for the contract to function and would have been included if the parties had given thought to the matter.

Two different tests can be used by the courts to determine whether a term should be implied:

- The business efficacy test
- The officious bystander test

The business efficacy test asks whether reasonable businessmen would have intended to include the term to ensure the efficacy of the contract (***The Moorcock [1899]***).

Scrutton LJ: *"An unexpressed term can only be implied if it is necessary in the business sense to give efficacy to the contract, i.e if it is such a term that it can confidently be said that if at the time the contract was being negotiated someone had said to the parties: 'What will happen in such a case' they would both have replied 'Of course, so and so will happen; we did not trouble to say that; it is too clear"* (**Reigate v Union Manufacturing Co (Ramsbottom) Ltd) *[1918]***).

The officious bystander test is that a term can be implied if an unrelated bystander is listening to the negotiations and would suggest to the parties that the term is included.

Mackinnon LJ defined this: *"That which in any contract is left to be implied and need not be expressed is something so obvious that it goes without saying; so that, if while the parties were making their bargain, an officious bystander were to suggest some express provision for it in their agreement, they would testily suppress him with a common 'Oh, of course!'"*

(***Shirlaw v Southern Foundaries [1926]***).

Lord Neuberger in ***Marks and Spencer plc v BNP Paribas Securities Services Trust Company (Jersey) Ltd. [2015]*** laid down the following criteria to determine whether the term should. Be implied.

- Reasonable people in the position of the parties would have put the term in
- A term should not be applied merely because it appears fair or because the parties would have incorporated it if it had been suggested to them
- Business necessity and obviousness should decide whether the term is implied
- The question to the officious bystander should be formulated with utmost care.

Terms can also be ***implied by law***. This happens when:

1) The contract is of a 'defined' type

   The contract is recognisable as a commonly occurring type of contract (such as an employment contract, sale contract, agency contract etc.).

2) The term is deemed necessary for that type of contract.

For instance, in ***Liverpool City Council v Irwin [1976]***, the Court held that the council who let out several apartments in one building had an implied obligation in law to ensure the common parts of the block were maintained in a reasonable state.

8. How are contractual terms incorporated?

There are four ways through which a term becomes part of the contract:

- By signature
- By notice
- Through course of dealing
- Through trade usage and custom

9. How is a term incorporated by signature?

In principle a party is bound by their signature. ***If someone signs a contract, they cannot later claim that they are not bound by the terms of the contract***. Even if they did not read the contract, they are still bound by the terms of the contract.

This is exemplified by the classic case of ***L'Estrange v Graucob [1934]***: Mrs L'Estrange owned a café and ordered a cigarette vending machine for her café. She signed the contract which stated she would be bound by the terms and conditions, but she did not read the terms which were in small print. One of these terms excluded any responsibility of the company for malfunctioning of the machine.

The machine arrived but did not work properly. Therefore, Mrs L'Estrange sued for the money she had already paid. The company stated that the contract she had signed made clear that the company excluded all liability and therefore she needed to pay regardless of whether the vending machine was actually working. The court agreed and held that it was immaterial whether Mrs L'Estrange had actually read the terms and she was bound by them anyway.

The general rule is therefore that ***any terms that have been signed are incorporated in the contract.*** This ensures certainty for the parties. If someone has signed it, they are bound by it. A signature carries an important legal value.

There are some exceptions:

Non Es Factum. If a party, without any fault on their part, could not understand the meaning of what they signed then the term would not be part of the contract. Think for instance of someone who is very ill when they sign or someone who does not know how to read.

The claimant must show two things:

(a) He was temporarily or permanently unable (through no fault of his own) to understand the nature of the document he signed

(b) There is a radical difference between what he signed and what he thought he was signing

Misrepresentation inducing a party to sign. If one of the parties mispresents the terms of the contract, then the term would not become part of the contract (***Curtis v Chemical Cleaning and Dyeing Co Ltd [1951]***) (for more on misrepresentation see Chapter X).

10. How is a term incorporated by notice?

There are three requirements:

- Notice should be given before or at the time of contracting.
- The terms must be contained in a contractual document.
- Reasonable steps must be taken to bring the notice to the attention of the other party; especially for unreasonable and onerous terms.

In ***Olley v Malborough Court Ltd [1949]*** a notice excluding the liability of the hotel for lost, stolen, or damaged property was placed in the hotel room. Mrs Olley was staying in the hotel and her coat was stolen from her room. She asked for damages to compensate her loss. The hotel refused saying they excluded liability for such losses. The court held that the notice was not incorporated in the contract because the guest would not see the notice until they got to their room and at that point, they would already have concluded the contract for their stay. Therefore, the notice was not part of the contract.

It is important to know when the contract is concluded to understand whether the term has become part of the contract. For instance, a ticket is seen as an offer which is accepted by the customer taking the ticket so a notice on the ticket would be part of the contract as this notice was given at the time of contracting (***Parker v South Eastern Railway [1877]***).

The terms should be contained in a contractual document which means that a receipt or similar type document would not be sufficient. Terms written on a receipt would not count as part of the contract. In ***Chapelton v Barry [1940]*** the claimant hired a deckchair and was injured. The receipt he received when hiring the chair contained an exclusion clause for injury. The court held that a reasonable person would not consider this receipt was a contractual document and therefore the term was not part of the contract.

Reasonable steps should be taken to bring the terms to the notice of the other party (***Parker v South Eastern Railway [1877]***), and the more unusual or onerous the terms are the more effort is required to bring these terms to the notice of the other party.

Not all steps need to be taken, just reasonable steps. For instance, there is no need to show the terms and conditions to the other party, it is in general enough to make the other party aware of their existence. For example, with a train ticket that referred to terms and conditions which were available on the timetables it was held that these were part of the contract even if the person buying the ticket would also need to purchase a timetable to be able to see them (***Thompson v London, Midland and Scottish Railway [1930]***). If the contract refers to a website where the terms are available this is also sufficient notice (***Impala Warehousing & Logistics Ltd v Wanxiang Resources Pte Ltd [2015]***).

However, if the terms are ***onerous or unreasonable*** then more steps should be taken. Lord Denning put it as follows: "*…the more unreasonable a clause is, the greater the notice which must be given of it. Some clauses which I have seen would need to be printed in red ink on the face of the document with a red hand pointing to it before the notice could be held to be sufficient.*" (***J Spurling Ltd v Bradshaw [1956]***).

In ***Interfoto Picture Library v Stiletto Visual Programmes [1989]***, Stiletto asked Interfoto to send them some photographs. Interfoto sent 47 transparencies in a jiffy bag along with a delivery note. The delivery note contained the terms and conditions. One of the terms said that if the transparencies were not returned by 19/3/1984 there was a fee of £5 per transparency per day until the transparencies were returned. Stiletto did not read the terms and they returned the transparencies late. The court held that the term was so onerous that more should have been done to bring this to the attention of Stiletto. Therefore, the term was not part of the contract.

11. How are terms incorporated through course of dealing, trade usages and custom?

Terms can be incorporated through ***course of dealing*** if the parties have contracted on a regular basis and are displaying consistent behaviour towards each other.

Example: Matthew, a carpenter, and Lucy, a forester, regularly do business with one another. They have never written down any terms for their arrangement. Every month Lucy comes by Matthew's place with a load of timber. She always leaves it in the front yard under a cover if Matthew is not in. Matthew always pays Lucy exactly one week after she delivers. If some pieces of timber are not of sufficient quality, Matthew alerts Lucy who then collects these pieces the next time she comes by.

Through their course of dealing the frequency of deliveries, the place of delivery, the time of payment, and the method to deal with timber of insufficient quality have become terms of the contract.

If Lucy one day decides she will no longer take back timber of insufficient quality and claims that she and Matthew never agreed that the timber should be of a certain quality, then the court will likely say that this term has become part of the contract through course of dealing.

Course of dealing should be consistent. In ***McCutcheon v David MacBrayne Ltd [1964]*** the claimant shipped his car with the defendant. The ship sank and so did the car. The parties had contracted on four previous occasions. Sometimes the claimant was asked to sign a note incorporating certain terms to exclude liability, but at other times he was not asked to do so. The defendant argued that the note was incorporated through course of dealing but the House of Lords did not agree because there was no consistent behaviour between the parties.

Course of dealing should also be regular. In ***Hollier v Rambler Motors [1972]*** the car of the claimant was damaged by a fire at the garage of the defendant. The claimant had used the garage 3 or 4 times over the last 5 years.

The previous occasions he had signed a form excluding liability, but this time they contracted over the phone and the claimant did not sign a form. The defendant said that the form was incorporated through course of dealing. The court said that 3-4 times in 5 years amounted to less than once a year and therefore there was no established course of dealing.

Terms are incorporated through custom and trade usages, if these are regular, consistent and well-known in the specific trade.

In ***British Crane Hire (BHC) Corporation v Ipswich Plant Hire (IPH) Ltd [1975]***, IPH hired a crane over the phone from BCH. BCH sent the terms of conditions, but IPH did not sign these. The crane sank in the marshland and BCH wanted IPH to pay for the crane, relying on an indemnity clause in the contract. IPH stated they did not sign the terms and were not bound by them. The court stated that indemnity clauses were standard in the crane hiring business and as IPH was in the trade they would have been aware of this usage and thus the term was incorporated in the contract.

12. What are standard clauses?

Contracts can be ***individually negotiated***: The parties negotiate the different clauses that make up the contract. This especially happens for specialist contracts and high value contracts.

Contracts can also consist of a mixture between ***individually negotiated clauses and standard terms***. Using standard terms saves time and money.

Contracts also consist ***entirely of standard clauses***. This is especially the case with low value, high volume contracts. These are also called adhesion contracts. They are drafted by the party who has the greater bargaining power, and the weaker party can adhere to the contract or reject it.

Standard clauses fall in two groups:

- Standard terms and conditions which businesses incorporate in all of their contracts
- Standard terms incorporated into a written contract (also called *boilerplate clauses*)

Boilerplate clauses are important because they save time, and it means that during the negotiations the parties can focus on key issues such as price, quality, quantity, and timing.

Summary:

- The terms of the contract determine the rights and obligations of the parties.
- Representations are statements made before entering into the contract, they are not part of the contract. If a representation is false. this leads to a claim for misrepresentation.
- The parol evidence rule states that when a contract is reduced into writing only what is written in the final contract document would be considered the terms of the contract. Any oral statements, emails, text messages, or other documents used in the negotiations are not part of the contract. This rule is a presumption and is rebuttable.
- Terms can be divided into express terms and implied terms.
- Implied terms are implied by statute, course of dealing, usage and custom, and by the court in fact or in law.
- Terms are incorporated in the contract through signature, notice, course of dealing, and usage and custom.

Problem Question:

Ticket Incorporation has hired Lucky Entertainment Ltd to find bands for a festival Ticket Incorporation is organising. During the negotiations Lucky Entertainment states, they will book Sound Collection for the festival. Sound Collection is one of the hottest new bands around. They are difficult to book but Lucky Entertainment Ltd reassures Ticket Incorporation that they have great connections, and it will be easy for them to book the band. Ticket Incorporation hires Lucky Entertainment and begins to advertise the festival stating that Sound Collection will perform. Tickets sell out very fast. However, the day of the festival Lucky Entertainment tells Ticket Incorporation that they were unable to book Sound Collection and instead True Blue will perform. True Blue plays the same genre, and they are very good, but they are also unknown. The attendees of the festival are disappointed because Sound Collection is not performing, and they want the money for their tickets back. Ticket Incorporation decides to sue Lucky Entertainment. Lucky Entertainment argues that they were hired to book bands which they did, and that Sound Collection's presence was not a term of the contract. The name Sound Collection is not in the contract

Is the presence of Sound Collection a term of the contract?

Given that the statement was made during the negotiations it could be either a representation or a term. To decide this all evidence should be taken into account: The timing of the statement (***Routledge v McKay [1954]***), the reassurances given by the other party (***Schawel v Reade [1913]***), the importance of the statement (***Bannerman v White [1861]***) and whether the statement was made by an expert (***Oscar Chess Ltd v Williams [1957]***). Given that Lucky Entertainment is in the business of booking bands they can be considered experts. Furthermore, they reassured Ticket Incorporation that they had the right connections and could book the band. Based on this it is likely that the statement will be held to be a term of the contract.

The parol evidence rule states that if an oral contract is reduced into writing all statements that are not written down are not contract terms. Therefore, Sound Collection's presence is not part of the contract. If it was so important the parties should have included this.

However, this rule is rebuttable so if Ticket Incorporation can show that the presence of Sound Collection was meant to be part of the contract then this would be a contractual term. Especially, if they can prove that the contract was dependent upon the presence of Sound Collection (***Pym v Campbell [1856]***). It could be that the promise is seen as a collateral contract (***J. Evans & Son (Portsmouth) v Andrea Merzario Ltd [1976]***) in which case booking Sound Collection was a collateral contract without which the main contract would not have been concluded.

Key Cases

Bannerman v White [1861] *10 CB NS 844*: the importance of the statement
Chapelton v Barry [1940] *1 KB 532*: notice should be contained in a contractual document
Cunliffe-Owen v Teather & Greenwood [1967] *1 WLR 1421*: custom must be notorious, certain, and reasonable
Curtis v Chemical Cleaning and Dyeing Co Ltd [1951] 1 K.B. 805: misrepresentation inducing a party to sign
Dick Bentley Productions Ltd v Harold Smith (Motors) Ltd [1965] *1 WLR 623:* if statement made by someone who is not an expert the statement is more likely to be a representation
Heilbut, Symons & Co v Buckleton [1913] *AC 30*: representation or term
Henderson v Arthur [1907] *1 KB 10*: written agreement trumps oral agreement
Hollier v Rambler Motors [1972] *2 QB 71*: course of dealing should be regular
Interfoto Picture Library v Stiletto Visual Programmes [1989] *QB 433:* the more onerous the notice the more steps should be taken to bring it to attention of the other party
J Spurling Ltd v Bradshaw [1956] 1 WLR 461: prominence of notice
J.Evans & Son (Portsmouth) v Andrea Merzario Ltd [1976] 1 WLR 1078: collateral contract
L'Estrange v Graucob [1934] *2 KB 394*: incorporation by signature
Marks and Spencer plc v BNP Paribas Securities Services Trust Company (Jersey) Ltd. [2015] UKSC 72: criteria to determine whether a term is necessary to imply
McCutcheon v David MacBrayne Ltd [1964] 1 WLR 125: consistency in course of dealing
Olley v Malborough Court Ltd [1949] 1 KB 532: timing of notice
Oscar Chess Ltd v Williams [1957] 1 WLR 370: statement made by an expert
Parker v South Eastern Railway [1877] 2 CPD 416: incorporation by notice
Pym v Campbell [1856] *6 EL & BL 370*: admissibility of external evidence
Rock Advertising Ltd v MWB Business Exchange Centres Ltd [2018] UKSC 24: oral variation of written

contract

Routledge v McKay [1954] *1 WLR 615*: the timing of the statement

Schawel v Reade [1913] *2 IR 81:* the strength of the statement

Smith v Wilson [1832] *110 ER 266*: qualifying a term under trade usage or custom

The Moorcock [1899] *14 P.D 64:* busines efficacy test

CHAPTER VIII

EXEMPTION CLAUSES AND UNFAIR TERMS

Learning Outcomes:

After reading this chapter, you should be able to understand:

- ✓ What exclusion and limitation clauses are;
- ✓ How incorporation and construction control the use of exemption clauses;
- ✓ The statutory provisions that control exemption clauses;
- ✓ How the law protects consumers against unfair contract terms.

Questions and Answers:

1. What are exclusion and limitation clauses?

They are clauses which exclude or restrict the liability of the parties to the contract and through which the parties seek to limit their losses. They are also called ***exemption clauses***.

Exclusion clauses seek to exclude, altogether, a party's liability for breaching the contract or a legal duty.

Limitation clauses seek to limit the extent of a party's liability for breaching the contract or a legal duty.

They can be viewed from two perspectives:

- They define the limits of the party's obligations and ensure the parties know the risks they incur under the contract.
- They seek to enable a party to escape or minimise liability for wrongdoing.

The use of exemption clauses is permitted, but the law imposes certain limits through:

- Controls at common law level.
- Statutory law.

The main statutory instrument is the ***Unfair Contract Terms Act 1977***.

There is a special statute for consumer contracts: ***The Consumer Rights Act 2015*** which incorporates the ***Unfair Terms in Consumer Contracts Regulation 1999***.

2. Is there a need to control exemption clauses?

Exemption clauses manage the extent of the risk contracting parties incur, help to keep prices low, make it possible for businesses to compete on a more level playing field, and protect the parties against unsustainable losses. The principle of freedom of contract suggests that the parties should be free to include exemption clauses in their contract.

However, as they allow a party to escape their contractual liability, this can mean that the other party ends up in a very disadvantaged position and could potentially incur substantial losses. This is especially true if we consider inequality of bargaining power between the parties. This would be the case for consumer contracts, but also in business contracts where there are significant imbalances between the contracting parties (for instance, if one of the parties is a multinational and the other is a SME (Small and Medium Enterprises).

Lord Reid said on exclusion clauses: "*In the ordinary way the customer has no time to read them, and if he did read them, he would probably not understand them. And if he did understand and object to any of them, he would generally be told he could take it or leave it. And if he then went to another supplier the result would be the same. Freedom to contract must surely imply some choice or room for bargaining.*" (***Suisse Atlantique SA v Rotterdamsche Kolencentrale NV [1967]***).

3. How are exemption clauses controlled at common law?

- *Incorporation*: Is the exclusion clause part of the contract?
- *Interpretation or construction:* Does the clause really exclude this specific liability?

For incorporation: See Chapter VII on Terms of the Contract.

4. How are terms constructed?

They are constructed ***contra profenterem***: against the party that is relying on the term.

Examples:

In ***Webster v Higging [1948]*** the contract included a term that read: *'no warranty, condition, description or representation is given or implied.'* The court said that as the term was formulated in the present tense it did not apply to oral warranties made before the contract was concluded.

In ***Houghton v Trafalgar Ins Co [1954]*** a car insurance policy excluded liability if the car was carrying an excessive load. The car was a five-seater and was carrying six people when it had an accident. The company argued that they were not liable because the load had been excessive. However, the Court of Appeal stated that 'load' should be given a narrow interpretation and refer to goods and not to people. Thus, the exclusion clause was not valid.

In response to cases like the above lawyers would draft exclusion clauses as wide as possible to cover all incidents whilst the courts would often try to construct the clauses so that these would not exclude liability for the particular incident to avoid unjust situations. This approach is not without its issues: 'too early recourse to the contra proferentem rule runs the danger of creating ambiguity where there is none' (***Direct Travel v McGeown [2003]***).

Whilst the same approach is used for exclusion as well as limitation clauses, the construction of limitation clauses should be less strict (***Ailsa Craig Fishing v Malvern Fishing [1983]***), depending on how extensive the limitation of liability.

5. What about clauses excluding liability for negligence?

The court developed a three-step approach for these in the case of ***Canada Steamship Lines Ltd v The King [1952]***:

1) If the clause refers to negligence directly or through a synonym the court will enforce this clause;

If not:

If the clause does not explicitly refer to negligence the court considers whether the ordinary meaning of the words is wide enough to cover negligence;

2) Could the exclusion clause cover another kind of liability than negligence, it will not be taken to cover negligence.

If step 1 is satisfied the court does not need to apply steps 2 or 3.

If step 1 is not satisfied both steps 2 and 3 must be applied.

This is referred to as ***the Canada Steamship test.***

6. How are exclusion clauses controlled through the Unfair Contract Terms Act 1977?

The Unfair Contract Terms Act 1977 (UCTA) was created because the judicial controls at common law level (incorporation and construction) were not fit for the purpose of avoiding unfairness. To avoid unfairness the court would sometimes construct clauses in an artificial manner, against the actual intentions of the parties. This case-by-case approach led to uncertainty and unpredictability. With the rise of standard contracts there was also a need to better protect weaker parties such as consumers. Furthermore, the contra profenterem rule can only prevent injustice up to a degree: If the clause has no ambiguity, it should be allowed.

Lord Denning in ***Georges Mitchell (Chesterhall) Ltd v Finney Lock Seeds Ltd [1982]*** referred to the difficulties with exemption clauses as 'the bleak winter for our law of contract' and to the construction approach as 'the secret weapon' which was followed by 'a spring of law reform' and summer in the form of the UCTA.

The UCTA applies to B2B contracts (Section 1(3)). Prior to 2015 it also applied to consumer contracts. You will therefore find a lot of caselaw pre 2015 where the UCTA was applied to consumer contracts. The UCTA does not apply to insurance, land, and intellectual property contracts and it does not apply to the formation/dissolution/constitution of a company. It applies to notices as well as contracts.

There are two methods through which exclusion clauses are controlled in the UCTA:

- Some exclusion clauses have no effect at all
- Other terms should satisfy a 'a test of reasonableness'

If a clause is wholly ineffective or held to be unreasonable then the term has no effect between the parties.

The decision of the court has no effect on other contracts containing similar terms.

7. Which exemption clauses have no effect at all?

Clauses that attempt to exclude or limit liability for death or personal injury caused by negligence have no effect (Section 2(1)). Negligence is the breach of any contractual obligation, any common law duty, and the common duty of care imposed by the Occupier's Liability Act 1957 to exercise reasonable skill and care (Section 1(1)).

8. What is the test of reasonableness?

Section 3 applies between contracting parties where one of them deals on the other's written standard terms of business (which means terms that are not individually negotiated).

A term cannot exclude/limit liability, endorse substantially different performance or non-performance unless it satisfies the test of

reasonableness. The test looks at the circumstances under which the parties entered into the contract and at the bargaining positions of the parties:

Schedule 2: "Guidelines" for Application of the Reasonableness Test:

(a)the strength of the bargaining positions of the parties relative to each other, taking into account (among other things) alternative means by which the customer's requirements could have been met;

(b)whether the customer received an inducement to agree to the term, or in accepting it had an opportunity of entering into a similar contract with other persons, but without having a similar term;

(c)whether the customer knew or ought reasonably to have known of the existence and the extent of the term (having regard, among other things, to any custom of the trade and any previous course of dealing between the parties);

(d)where the term excludes or restricts any relevant liability if some condition was not complied with, whether it was reasonable at the time of the contract to expect that compliance with that condition would be practicable;

(e)whether the goods were manufactured, processed or adapted to the special order of the customer.

The strength of each element of the guidelines depends on the facts of the case. The test does not look at the content of the exclusion clauses as much as at the circumstances under which the term became part of the contract.

Liability for implied terms under statutes such as the Sale of Goods Act 1979 cannot be excluded unless this meets the test of reasonableness.

For speciality contracts (carriage of goods, employment…) specific rules exist on the type of liability that might be excluded from the contract

The court should also take in consideration ***whether the contract is covered by insurance*** (***Smith v Bush [1990]***).

8. How has caselaw developed since the UCTA?

The UCTA did not abolish the judicial controls at common law. However, there is now less need for an elaborate construction of exclusion clauses. The contra proferentem rule should only apply if the parties' objective intention cannot be ascertained from how the clause is worded in the context of the contract and only if the wording is genuinely ambiguous (***Transocean Drilling UK Ltd v Providence Resources plc [2016]***). Older cases should be read in a more contextual approach (***Whitecap Leisure Ltd v John H Rundle Ltd [2008]***). Interpretation should reflect 'commercial common sense' and be straightforward with 'judicial creativity' only invoked to 'remedy a widespread injustice' (***BCCI SA* v *Ali [2001]***).

The Canada Steamship test continues to apply but should be seen more as guidance rather that it always needs to be strictly followed (***HIH Casualty and General Insurance Ltd v Chase Manhattan Bank [2003]***).

9. What is the law with regards to consumer contracts?

In 1994 the UK incorporated the EU Directive on Unfair Terms in Consumer Contracts 93/13/EC: The Unfair Terms in Consumer Contracts Regulations 1994 (UTCCR) which was updated in 1999. Between 1994 and 2015 both the UCTA and UTCCR were applicable to consumer contracts. There was an overlap between both instruments.

In 2015 the UTCCR was replaced by Section 2 of the Consumer Rights Act (CRA) 2015. The case law under the UTCCR remains relevant because the provisions of the Regulation have become part of the act. The case law of the ECJ also remains important for any cases prior to Brexit.

The UCTA 1977 was applicable to consumer contracts before 2015. Since 2015 the UCTA is no longer applicable to consumer contracts and exemptions clauses in consumer contracts are regulated by the CRA.

10. What are the key things to know about the CRA?

First it is important to know that the UCTA only applies to exemption clauses whereas ***the CRA applies to any term of the contract other than those that define the main subject matter of the contract and those that determine the price***. Therefore, the CRA has a broader remit in the terms that it covers than the UCTA.

The CRA is applicable to B2C contracts and applies to notices as well as contracts.

A trader is defined in the CRA as *'a person acting for purposes relating to that person's trade, business, craft or profession whether acting personally or through another person acting in the trader's name or on the trader's behalf.'* Business includes the activities of any government department, local or public authorities.

A consumer is defined in the CRA as an *'individual acting for purposes that are wholly or mainly outside the individual's trade, business, craft, or profession.'*

The CRA does not apply to employment or apprenticeship contracts.

Under the CRA a trader cannot exclude liability for death or personal injury resulting from negligence (Section 65). Personal injury is defined as any disease and any impairment of physical or mental condition.

The trader can also not exclude or limit liability rising from terms implied into the contract by the Act which includes:

- Terms implied into contracts for the sale of goods (Section 31)
- Terms implied into contracts for the supply of services (Section 57)
- Terms implied into contracts for the sale of digital content (Section 47)

Whilst in this chapter we are concerned with part 2 of the CRA regarding unfair contract terms it should be noted that the CRA also contains other provisions on consumer contracts. Part 1 of the CRA covers general provisions for consumer contracts for goods, digital content, and services whereas part 3 covers several miscellaneous provisions with regards to secondary ticketing (reselling tickets) and the duties of letting agents on the publication of fees among others.[4]

11. When is a term unfair?

There are two elements to ***the test of fairness*** (Section 62):

- The term or the notice is contrary to the requirement of good faith.
- The term or the notice causes a significant imbalance in the parties' rights and obligations to the detriment of the consumer.

The court should give weight to the subject matter of the contract and the context of the contract when deciding whether the term is unfair. A term is more likely unfair if it is one-sided or has not been brought sufficiently to the attention of the consumer. A term is more likely fair if the consumer has substantial knowledge and experience of the subject matter and of the risks he might incur because of the term.

To decide whether there is a ***significant imbalance*** the content of the term should be examined carefully. This is not only aimed at procedural unfairness (how the term became part of the contract) but also substantial unfairness (what the term says). This is different from the UCTA which mainly looks at procedural unfairness.

The court looks at the extent to which the consumer is deprived of a legal right and whether the consumer would have chosen to incorporate that term if they

[4] You can find the CRA here: https://www.legislation.gov.uk/ukpga/2015/15/contents/enacted

could have negotiated the contract individually (***Aziz v Caixa d'Estalvis de Catalunya, Tragno I Maresea [2013]***). Lord Bingham stated: "*the requirement of significant imbalance is met if a term is so weighted in favour of the supplier as to tilt the parties' rights and obligations under the contract significantly in his favour*" (***Director General of Fair Trading v First National Bank [2001]***).

There are three views on ***the requirement of good faith***:

1) Good faith has no independent role – good faith is a tool that helps to determine whether there is a significant imbalance between the parties.
2) Significant imbalance is the threshold requirement and good faith should be applied to any cases that do not meet the threshold.
3) Good faith and significant imbalance are both important and should be applied together.

The third view is the most prevalent.

In ***Director General of Fair Trading v First National Bank [2001]*** Lord Bingham defined good faith as open and fair dealing and that it looks to good standards of commercial morality and practice. He stated that ***terms should be expressed fully, clearly and legible***. Prominence should be given to terms which might be disadvantageous for the consumer and a trader should not take advantage of the consumer's necessity, lack of experience, unfamiliarity, and weak bargaining position. In the same case Lord Steyn said good faith is an objective criterion which implies fair and equitable dealing.

In ***ParkingEye Ltd v Beavis [2015]*** the Court looked at whether a penalty term could be seen as unfair. Mr Beavis had parked his car in a retail park where he could park for free for two hours. However, if a customer stayed longer than two hours, he would have to pay £85 in parking charges as could be read on notices around the carpark. Mr Beavis overstayed and refused to pay the charge because he thought it was unfair as ParkingEye had not suffered a loss of £85. ParkingEye argued was that there was a commercial justification as the term would deter motorists staying longer and therefore ensured accessibility of the retail park. The courts considered the effect of the term, the legitimate interest of the company, and whether the term went beyond what is necessary. The Supreme Court stated that whilst there was an imbalance in the rights between the parties the term was not contrary to the requirements of good faith because ParkingEye had a legitimate interest in ensuring the carpark stayed available for other customers, the charges were its only source of income, the notices were clear and transparent, the consumer could leave without any issue when he saw the notice, and a reasonable motorist would have agreed with the incorporation of the term.

All terms should be transparent which means that the term is 'expressed in plain and intelligible language and is legible' (Section 68(2)).

12. What happens when a term is unfair?

An unfair term of a consumer contract is not binding on the consumer. The contract is still valid, but the specific term would not bind the consumer. The term is treated as if it never existed. The court cannot re-write the term to make it 'fairer' so the contract will continue to exist without the term, unless the contract cannot exist without this term and then the contract will be ended (***C-118/17 Dunai v ERSTE Bank Hungary Zrt [2019]***).

Whilst the trader cannot rely on the term, the consumer can rely on the term if they choose to do so. The above also applies to unfair notices.

If the court finds a term unfair in a ***general challenge*** it will not be enforceable in any future contracts and where appropriate also not in current contracts. Therefore, ***the decision of the court is not limited to the specific case, but to all contracts containing the term.***

13. Which terms are excluded from the CRA?

The fairness of a term defining ***the main subject matter of the contract*** cannot be challenged. This concerns the essential obligation of the contract. This is usually constructed narrowly. In ***OFT v Ashbourne Management Services* Ltd *[2011]*** a gym imposed a minimum membership period of one to three years. If a person chose to quit their membership early, they would need to continue to pay until the end of the minimum period. The question was whether the membership period was part of the subject matter of the contract and therefore could not be challenged for fairness. The court disagreed and stated that the term did not define the subject matter of the contract as the dispute was about charges for early termination. The term could therefore be challenged and was found to be unfair for a period beyond one year.

A price term is in principle not seen as unfair because it is regulated by the market, and competition law should ensure there is a level playing field so that prices are not artificially high. Therefore, under the CRA these terms cannot be challenged for unfairness.

This only applies if the term is:

- **transparent** (expressed in plain and intelligible language & legible);
    - **prominent** (brought to the consumer's awareness in such a way that the average consumer would be aware of the term).

(The average consumer is a person who is reasonably well informed, observant, and circumspect) (Section 64).

In ***Director General of Fair Trading v First National Bank [2001]*** a loan agreement contained a term that if the client defaulted on the repayment the bank would be entitled to recover the complete loan and any outstanding interest from the client's bank account. The bank argued that this term concerned the adequacy of price and was thus excluded from assessment for fairness. The House of Lords rejected the defence of the bank and stated this was not a core price term and that exclusion of price terms should be given a restrictive interpretation: "*After all, in a broad sense all terms of the contract are in some way related to the price or remuneration. That is not what is intended.... It would be a gaping hole in the system if such clauses were not subject to the fairness requirement*" (Lord Steyn). The term could therefore be assessed for fairness, and the House of Lords ultimately considered the term fair.

This can be contrasted with ***Office of Fair Trading v Abbey National plc [2009]*** where a term regarding charges on authorised overdrafts was considered to be a price term and therefore could not be challenged. This has the effect of limiting the application of ***Director General of Fair Trading v First National Bank [2001].*** The difference was that the overdraft charge in ***First National*** was a result of a breach of payment terms whereas the interest on overdrafts in ***Abbey National*** was considered the price for the service of having an overdraft.

14. What is the role of the competent competition market authorities?

For consumers is difficult to challenge the fairness of terms because this takes time, money, and knowledge. Therefore, ***the CRA allows for competent market authorities to challenge unfair terms of the contract.*** Often cases do not end in court because the regulator will negotiate with the business to change or drop the term. As companies also wish to avoid court cases these negotiations are often successful.

The main regulator is the Competition and Market Authority (CMA) (formerly Office of Fair Trading). They are not the sole regulator. Others include:

- Department of Enterprise, Trade and Investment in Northern Ireland
- The Financial Conduct Authority
- The Office of Communications
- The Gas and Electricity Markets Authority
- The Office of Rail Regulation
- The Consumers' Association…

(See Paragraph 8 of Schedule 3 for the full list).

Regulators other than the CMA must inform the CMA that they intent to investigate a term. The Regulator can make an application for injunction and if they refuse to do so they must give reason to the person who made the complaint. Regulators have investigatory powers.

The court should be pro-active and consider the issue of fairness of the term even if none of the parties raises this issue as part of the court proceedings (Section 71).

15. What is the grey list?

Schedule 2 of the CRA contains a grey list of terms that have the potential to be unfair. ***These terms are allowed but should bear further scrutiny as they are likely to be unfair.***

This includes terms which:

- Exclude/limit liability for personal injury or death (for other reasons than negligence).
- Exclude/limit the legal rights of the consumer in relation to the trader or another party in the event of non-performance or inadequate performance.
- Bind the consumer to the contract before binding the trader.
- Require a consumer to pay a disproportionate high amount of compensation in case of non-performance or non-conclusion.
- Allow the trader to dissolve the contract on a discretionary basis whilst not allowing the consumer to do the same.
- Enable a trader to terminate the contract without reasonable notice.
- Automatically extend a contract of fixed duration.
- Enable the trader to alter the terms and conditions of the contract unilaterally without a specified reason.
- Allow the trader to alter the characteristics of the subject matter, goods, or services.
- Give the trader discretion to decide or raise the price after the conclusion, without giving the consumer the right to cancel the contract.
- Let the trader decide whether the goods conform to the contract.
- Oblige the consumer to fulfil his obligations without reciprocity.
- Limit warranties for the consumer without the consumers agreement.
- Hinder or excludes the consumer's right to exercise a legal remedy.

Summary:

Judicial controls at common law:

- Incorporation.
- Construction: contra profenterem (against who is relying on the term).
- Exclusion of damage caused by negligence should satisfy the Canada Steamship Test.

Statutory Control:

- Unfair Contract Terms Act 1977 (since 2015 only applicable to B2B contracts).
- Consumer Rights Act 2015 (incorporates Unfair Contract Terms Regulation 1993/1999).

UCTA 1977:

- Liability for personal injury/death through negligence cannot be excluded.
- If dealing on standard terms the exclusion clause should satisfy a test of reasonableness.
- Test of reasonableness focuses on procedural fairness.
- Only applies to the specific case and contract that is challenged.

CRA 2015:

- Liability for personal injury/death through negligence cannot be excluded.
- Other terms are subject to the test of fairness.
- The term should not be contrary to good faith and not cause a significant imbalance to the rights of the parties.
- Focus on both procedural and substantive fairness.
- Price terms and terms defining main subject matter excluded from assessment.
- Competent market authorities can challenge terms.
- Includes a grey list with potential unfair terms.

Problem Question:

Global Industry Solutions (GIS) has contracted with Titan Computers to buy and install 500 computers. Within a week of instalment two of the computers explode injuring a member of staff. The cause of this was faulty instalment. Furthermore, there appears to be a virus in the system which has affected some of the software used by GIS. The whole system needs to be taken offline and reinstalled which takes several days. This not only costs money but also means that the company loses valuable sales over those days.

The written agreement between the two companies contains the following clause:

> *Titan Computers will not be liable for any loss or damage sustained or incurred by the Customer (including without limitation any loss of use of the Products or loss of or spoiling of any of the Customer's programs or data) resulting from any fault in the Products. This includes instances of death or personal injury.*
>
> *Titan Computers total liability to the Customer under these Terms and Conditions if the product is faulty is limited to the amount paid by the Customer for the relevant Services (which gives rise to the claim) purchased by the Customer.*
>
> *Notwithstanding anything else contained in these Terms and Conditions, Titan Industries will not be liable to the Customer for loss of business, profits or contracts or other indirect or consequential loss whether arising from negligence, breach of contract or any other means.*

Is Titan Computers able to rely on this clause to exclude liability?

First, it is important to establish whether the term was incorporated in the contract. This is done through signature, by notice, through course of dealing, or custom.

In this instance, the term is part of a written agreement and is incorporated through signature (***L'Estrange v E. Graucob Ltd [1934]***). This is likely a standard term of Titan Computers.

The next step would be to look at two issues:

1) Is the term allowed under statutory law?
2) Constructing the term under the contract.

Since the UCTA came into existence the construction of the term should only be done if there is genuine ambiguity as to the meaning of the term (***Transocean Drilling UK Ltd v Providence Resources plc [2016]***). Nevertheless, the wording of the clause must be read carefully to see whether it actually excludes the damage that has occurred. The damage that has occurred is:

1) Personal injury of staff member.
2) Damage to equipment that was bought under the contract.
3) Damage to software and need to reinstall the system.
4) Loss of income because of lost sales.

What does the term exclude/limit?

1) Personal injury.

2) Damage to the software.
3) Loss of equipment.

Titan Industries does not exclude the damage to the computers as long as the total amount does not exceed the price that was paid for them. Therefore, there are three contested claims which based on the wording of the claim seem to be excluded by the contract.

Is the term allowed under the UCTA?

The exclusion of liability for personal injury because of negligence is not allowed under the UCTA (Section 2(1)). If GIS can prove that the faulty instalment was caused by negligence, Titan Computers would be responsible.

The remainder of the clause would have to satisfy the reasonableness test if this term is part of the standard terms and conditions (Section 3). Based on the wording of the clause it is hard to say whether the clause satisfies the reasonableness test. This is because the reasonableness test looks mainly to the circumstances under which the term became part of the contract (Schedule 2). Therefore, we would need to know the respective bargaining positions of both parties and the other facts surrounding the case.

Titan Industries would be liable for:

1) Personal injury of staff member if negligence is established.
2) Damage to the equipment that was bought under the contract (the computers) as this is not excluded under the contract.

They might be liable for:

1) Damage to software and need to reinstall the system.
2) Loss of income because of lost sales.

This depends on whether the term meets the test of reasonableness and to know this we need to know the circumstances under which the parties contracted.

Key Cases

Ailsa Craig Fishing v Malvern Fishing [1983]1 WLR 964: construction of limitation clauses

Andrew Bros etc. v Singer etc. [1934] 1 KB 17 (CA): contra profenterem construction

Aziz v Caixa d'Estalvis de Catalunya, Tragno I Maresea [2013] *Case C-415/1*: how far does the term deprive the consumer of his rights

BCCI SA v Ali [2001] *UKHL 8*: interpretation should reflect commercial common sense

Canada Steamship Lines Ltd v The King [1952] UKPC 1: Canada Steamship Test,

Director General of Fair Trading v First National Bank [2001] *UKHL 52*:key case on price terms in consumer contracts, defines requirements of fairness test in detail

Georges Mitchell (Chesterhall) Ltd v Finney Lock Seeds Ltd [1982] *EWCA Civ 5*: Unsuitability of construction approach to control exemption clauses

HIH Casualty and General Insurance Ltd v Chase Manhattan Bank [2003] *UKHL 6*: Canada Steamship Test continues to apply, but should be seen more as guidelines
Houghton v Trafalgar Ins Co [1954] *1 QB 247:* contra profenterem construction of terms
Office of Fair Trading v Abbey National Plc [2009] UKSC 6: price terms
ParkingEye Ltd v Beavis [2015] UKSC 67: legitimate interest
Smith v Bush [1990] *UKHL 1*: presence of insurance
Suisse Atlantique SA v Rotterdamsche Kolencentrale NV [1967] *AC 361*: highlights issues with exclusion clauses in consumer contracts
Transocean Drilling UK Ltd v Providence Resources plc [2016] *EWCA Civ 372*: contra profenterem rule should be applied if parties' objective intention cannot be ascertained
Webster v Higging [1948] *2 All E.R 127*: contra profenterem construction of exclusion clause

CHAPTER IX

DURESS AND UNDUE INFLUENCE

Learning Outcomes:

After reading this chapter, you should be able to understand:

- ✓ The different categories of duress: duress of the person, economic duress, and duress of goods;
- ✓ The necessary elements of duress;
- ✓ The classes of undue influence: actual undue influence and presumed undue influence;
- ✓ How undue influence is established.

Questions and Answers

1. How does the law protect against unfair bargaining?

Parties often have unequal bargaining powers. Furthermore, coming to an agreement might be much more important for one of the parties than for the other(s). Parties often use their economic powers to get a better deal. In principle, there is nothing wrong with using one's stronger commercial position to come to a more favourable agreement for oneself. However, the law does place limits on how that power is used. Contract law is founded on freedom of contract and the freely given consent of the parties to be bound by the contract. Therefore, if there is a factor that vitiates that consent this could invalidate the contract.

Limits on how a contracting party can use their power are set through the doctrines of:

- Duress
- Undue influence

Statutory law also lists certain prohibited practices with regards to the behaviour of the parties, such as for consumer contracts under the Consumer Protection from Unfair Trading Regulations 2008.

There is no overall doctrine in English contract law on unfair bargaining and the principle of ***unconscionability*** has limited recognition.

2. What is duress?

Duress can be defined as getting someone to agree to enter into a contract through violence, a threat of violence, or other illegitimate pressure. Duress is a vitiating factor and can make a contract voidable.

There are three types of duress:

- Duress of the person
- Duress of goods
- Economic duress

The conditions for duress are:

- There must be some illegitimate pressure exerted on the contracting party.
- This pressure induced the contracting party to agree.
- The contracting party had no real choice but to agree because there was no reasonable alternative course of action.
- The contracting party protested within a reasonable time after the duress stopped.

This list is not exhaustive and duress cases are heavily determined by the facts of the case.

Earlier cases use the concept of 'coercion of the will.' The idea is that because of the duress, the contracting party is no longer acting out of their free will but instead is 'forced' to agree. Later case law nuances this concept. Even if a person is acting under duress, they still have a choice, and their will is not overborne (***Lynch v DPP of Northern Ireland [1975]***).[5] The law now focuses on the lack of 'an alternative remedy which a reasonable person would have pursued' (***Hoyton SA v Peter Cremer GmbH [1999]***).

Example: Alfie threatens Lina at gunpoint to give her bike to Alfie and in exchange he will give her £5 and won't hurt her. Lina agrees. Lina made a conscious choice to give Alfie what he wanted to avoid getting hurt. She could have chosen to take the risk and hope Alfie was bluffing. She still had free will. However, that was clearly not a reasonable alternative. Lina made the decision to say yes to Alfie because there was no real alternative.

Duress focuses on the behaviour of both parties:

- Legitimacy of the pressure of the alleged wrongdoer

---

[5] See also P. Atiyah, 'Economic Duress and the Overborne Will', (1982) 98 LQR 197.

- Effect of pressure on the alleged victim.

4. What is duress of the person?

This is the oldest form of duress and traditionally the only form that was recognised under the common law. It means that there should be ***an act of violence or a threat of violence against the contracting party or someone closely associated with them*** such as a family member. The threat of violence does not need to be the sole factor that induced the victim into entering the contract.

In ***Barton v Armstrong [1976]***, Mr Armstrong was the chairman and shareholder of a company. Mr Barton was the managing director and shareholder of the same company. Barton was unhappy with the way that the company was run by Armstrong, and he wanted him removed from office. Armstrong refused to leave. Barton and the other directors removed all credit facilities from the company to put pressure on Armstrong to leave. Armstrong discovered this, and he made death threats against Barton and pressured Barton into signing a contract buying Armstrong's shares for more money than they were worth. The company became insolvent shortly after and Barton sought to have the contract set aside. The Privy Council agreed that Barton was coerced into the contract. He might have agreed to the contract even without the threats because it got him the result that he wanted which was that Armstrong would be gone from the company. However, as the threats would have played at least a role in his decision to sign the contract, Barton was successful in his claim and the contract could be set aside for duress.

Even if the deal is objectively a good one, the presence of duress can make the contract voidable.

For instance: Ilyas is selling his house. His house is worth £300,000. Pietro wants to buy Ilyas's house for £350,000 and says that he will kill Ilyas if Ilyas does not sell to him. Ilyas signs the contract and sells to Pietro. Whilst Pietro paid a more than fair price for the house and Ilyas wanted to sell the house anyway, Ilyas can still have the contract set aside for duress because his agreement was obtained under threats of violence.

4. What is duress of goods?

Duress of goods is a contested category of duress. It means that ***a threat is made against the goods of the contracting partner to ensure his agreement.***

Example: Arlen has asked Sifra to fix his computer in exchange for £300. Sifra agrees and fixes the computer. After the repairs are done Sifra tells Arlen the actual cost is £350. Sifra says that if he does not pay, she will not give him back his computer and the books he forgot at her shop when he brought the computer in. Arlen agrees because he really wants his computer and books back. Sifra's threats were not against Arlen, but against Arlen's goods. Therefore, this is duress of goods.

The leading authority is ***Skeate v Beale [1841]***. Mr Beale rented a house from Mr Skeate. He was behind on his payments. Mr Skeate confiscated some goods from Mr Beale and threatened to sell these goods. Mr Beale agreed to a repayment scheme for the rent. He then sought to have the contract set aside for duress. The court held that duress of goods was not sufficient to set aside the contract.

If someone's goods are being threatened this is unfortunate for the person, but in principle this is not enough pressure for someone to agree to enter into a contract against their will. That person could also go to court and start an action to have their goods released. The threat against their possessions is not enough to vitiate their consent.

Therefore, duress of goods was not recognised as a vitiating factor. ***The courts now seem willing to recognise duress of goods,*** but there are as of yet no clear authorities on this issue. ***Skeate v Beale*** predates the recognition of economic duress so the courts would likely take a different decision now.

In ***Occidental Worldwide Investment v Skibs (The Sibeon & The Sibotre) [1976]*** Kerr Justice stated in his obiter dictum: *"If I should be compelled to sign a lease or some other contract for a nominal but legally sufficient consideration under an imminent threat of having my house burnt down or a valuable picture slashed through without any threat of physical violence to anyone, I do not think that the law would uphold the agreement."*

This seems a clear indication that duress of goods should be recognised. In ***Dimskal Shipping v ITWF (The Evia Luck) [1991]*** Lord Goff made reference to ***Skeate v Beale*** no longer being good law. However, there is no clear authority yet that overrules ***Skeate v Beale***.

It is worth noting that in ***restitution claims***, duress of goods is recognised (***Astley v Reynolds [1731]*** **and** ***Maskell v Horner [1915]***).

5. What is economic duress?

This is ***economic pressure that is applied illegitimately to induce someone to enter into a contract.*** This category of duress has been recognised since the 1970s. ***Mere commercial pressure is not considered enough to amount to duress.*** In almost all contractual relations there will be some form of commercial/economic pressure. However, when that commercial pressure becomes illegitimate this constitutes economic duress. Threats made under economic duress do not incite violence but include threatened breach or cancellation of contract, boycotts, cancelled deliveries etc. It is key to consider the acceptability of economic pressure from the perspective of a commercial relationship and how the business world, where hard bargaining is the norm, views such pressure.

Dyson J in ***DSDN Subsea Ltd v Petroleum Geoservices ASA [2000]***: *"The ingredients of actionable duress are that there must be pressure, (a) whose practical effect is that there is compulsion on, or a lack of practical choice for the victim, (b) which is illegitimate and(c) which is a significant cause inducing the claimant to enter into the contract."*

Economic duress was first recognised in ***Occidental Worldwide Investment v Skibs (The Sibeon & The Sibotre) [1976]***. The first case that applied economic duress was ***North Ocean Shipping Co v Hyundai Construction Co (The Atlantic Baron) [1979]***. A contract for the building of a ship was concluded. After conclusion, the sellers wanted to raise the price by 10%. The buyers agreed because they had already chartered the ship to an oil company, and they therefore needed the ship in their possession so they could honour that contract. 8 months after delivery, they sued and claimed back the extra 10%. The court agreed that the pressure applied constituted economic duress, but that because of the time lapse (laches) the buyers could not recover the 10%.

Universe Tankships v International Transport Workers' Federation (The Universe Sentinel) [1983] represents the move away from the coercion of the will theory to establish duress. In an industrial dispute, the International Transport Workers Federation blocked a ship (The Universe Sentinel) from leaving port. The Federation made several demands with regard to pay and conditions for the sailors. They also demanded that the owners of the ship pay a sum of money to a welfare fund for sailors. The owners agreed as they needed the ship unblocked to ensure they could meet their contractual obligations. The owners then protested the welfare payment. The court held that the contribution to the fund was made under economic duress. Striking for better pay and conditions is not illegal but asking for a contribution to the welfare fund was seen as problematic because it did not fell under the legal remit of the strike.

The court focused on two necessary elements for establishing duress:

1) Absence of choice or an alternative for the contracting party.
2) Illegitimacy of the pressure applied to the contracting party.

6. When does duress occur?

Duress occurs mainly between ***parties that already are in a contractual relationship***. It often involves one of the parties asking for a variation of contract or for further concessions.

Whilst commercial pressure also exists at the time of contractual negotiations this would only under very rare circumstances be recognised as duress. Freedom of contract ensures that ***the parties have the right to freely withdraw from negotiations, introduce new terms in the contract, or make other significant changes right up until the contract is concluded*** (***Bank of India v Riat [2014]***).

There is also a difference between threatening to breach a contract or threatening to not contract again in the future. The first is much more likely to meet the threshold of duress: *"A threat to break a contract will generally be regarded as illegitimate, particularly where the defendant must know that it would be in breach of contract if the threat was implemented"* (***Kolmar Group AG V Traxpo Enterprises Pvt Ltd [2010]***).

Atlas Express Ltd v Kafco (Importers & Distributors) Ltd [1989] focused on threatened breach of contract. Kafco imported baskets and had a lucrative contract with the retail chain Woolworths that bought the baskets from Kafco. Atlas Express delivered the baskets to Woolworths and threatened to breach the contract with Kafco unless they got more money for delivery. Kafco agreed but never paid the extra money. Atlas Express went to court and Kafco used economic duress as a defence. The court held that there was economic duress because there was no alternative option open for Kafco. If they had not agreed and Atlas Express had breached the contract, Kafco could have gone to court for damages. However, this would have left them without a delivery company, and they would therefore not have been able to fulfil their contract with Woolworths. This would have significant financial consequences for Kafco and they therefore had no practical choice but to agree to the variation in contract.

7. When is pressure illegitimate?

In contractual bargaining, there is often commercial pressure. This is legitimate. It can be difficult to define exactly when pressure is illegitimate.

- A threat to do an unlawful act is always illegitimate.
- A threat to do a lawful act will be illegitimate if the threat is unreasonable.

Two examples:

B&S Contracts and Design Ltd v Victor Green Publications Lt [1984]: The employees of a company contracted to build stands for an exhibition threatened to go on strike unless they were paid a lump sum. The company asked the organisers of the conference to pay half the sum which they did. After the completion of the work, the organisers deducted this sum to the payment owed to the company. The company sued the organisers. The court held that there was duress because if the organisers had not paid the money the work would not be completed, and the exhibition could not go ahead leaving the organisers liable for a myriad of claims arising out of other contracts.

Here, the threat was seen as unlawful because of ***the lack of a reasonable alternative*** for the organisers and the heavy economic damage they would suffer if they did not agree. Of course, the organisers could have found other contractors to build the stands but there likely would not have been enough time for this.

R v Attorney General for England and Wales [2003]: Members of the SAS published books on the SAS Bravo Two Zero Patrol. This led to the Ministry of Defence introducing a confidentiality agreement to be signed by all SAS Members. R was told that if he did not sign the contract, he would be transferred and so he signed. When he retired, he wrote his memoirs. He was sued for breach of the confidentiality agreement. One of R's defences was duress: He had signed the contract because he would be transferred which he did not want as being a member of the SAS is prestigious and pays better. The Court held that the Ministry of Defence was entitled to transfer a soldier to another unit and thus the threat to return R to his old regiment was lawful.

It should be noted that this was not a commercial case and therefore does not fit well in any of the established categories of duress. This demonstrates that ***the law has broadened its perspective on when duress can occur, and that the categories are not exhaustive***. Whilst the court in this case did not recognise the duress, the court also did not state that duress could not occur in this type of employment relationship.

Informing a party of their existing liabilities under the contract is not considered illegitimate pressure (***Berntsen v National Westminster Bank [2012]***).

Example: Bernadette has given a loan to Cisco. In the contract it is specified that if Cisco does not pay back Bernadette before the 31st of July, he needs to give his car to Bernadette. If Bernadette reminds Cisco of this clause, it will put pressure on Cisco who might feel anxious and stressed. However, that pressure is not illegitimate.

This is also the case if the party believes in good faith that their demand is legitimate, even if it is not (***CTN Cash & Carry Ltd v Gallagher Ltd [1994]***).

The victim must come forward once the duress has stopped. If they wait too long, then even if the duress is proven the contract cannot be set aside anymore (***The Atlantic Barron [1979]***).

The protestations of the victim at the time of the conclusion of the contract can be taken into account but it should be understood that if there is duress the victim might not have a choice but to agree, lest they face financial ruin. They might not protest too much because of this (***Kolmar Group AG v Traxpo Enterprises Pvt Ltd [2010]***).

The above gives an indication as to the conditions necessary to prove economic duress, but it should be emphasised that the law is not settled as Tomlinson LJ stated in ***Lupo Fresh Limited v Sapporo Breweries Limited [2013]***: *"Economic duress is an emerging doctrine, the bounds of which can by no means be regarded as yet settled."*

7. How does the court see inducement?

For duress of the person, the causal link between the duress and the agreement can be very low. If someone made a violent threat you do not have to prove that this was the main reason why you entered into the contract. Think of ***Barton v Armstrong [1976]*** whereby what Armstrong offered Barton was something that Barton had wanted in the first place (albeit at a lower price) and is not unlikely Barton would have agreed even without the threats. However, threats were made by Armstrong and that was enough to prove causation.

For economic duress, the threshold of causation is higher, and the alleged victim of duress must prove that the duress was the main reason in his decision to agree to the contract. In ***Huyton SA v Peter Cremer GmbH & Co [1999]*** Lord Mance said that the proper test is the 'but for' test (*sine qua non*).

The 'but for' test has become increasingly important in deciding whether there was economic duress and has taken some of the focus away from the lack of a reasonable alternative (***Sheikh Tahnoon v Ioannis Kent [2018]***).

8. What is undue influence?

Before the 1970s only duress against the person was recognised. This was a very high threshold to meet as luckily violent threats are not that common in contractual negotiations. The high threshold left many people without recourse to a legal remedy even if they felt pressured to enter into a contract.

Out of response to the high threshold of the common law duress doctrine, undue influence developed in ***equity*** to give people a recourse. Because undue influence is a creature of equity its principles are less strictly formed and applied than those of common law doctrines.

It is perfectly normal for people to influence one another or to give each other advice. However, if the relationship between the parties is an unequal one or if one of the parties has a strong hold over the other party that influence can be undue. ***Undue influence means that one party influences the other by taking advantage of their relationship or the position of the other in such a way that this is not considered acceptable.***

Both the behaviour of the alleged perpetuator and the state of mind of the alleged victim play a role in deciding whether there was undue influence: Lord Millet: "*The doctrine involves two elements. First, there must be a relationship capable of giving rise to the necessary influence. And secondly the influence generated by the relationship must have been abused*" (***National Commercial Bank (Jamaica) Ltd v Hew [2003]***).

9. What are the classes of undue influence?

Class 1

Actual undue influence: The application of illegitimate pressure upon a party to induce them to agree.

Class 2

Presumed undue influence: Taking advantage of a relationship of trust and confidence to the detriment of the other party.

Presumed undue influence is broken down into two further categories:

a) Relationships in which the law presumes that one party was in a position to exercise influence over the other (doctor-patient, parent- minor child, guardian-ward, solicitor-client, religious leader-follower…).

b) Cases in which the claimant can prove there was a relationship of trust and confidence even if it does not fall in the recognised categories of 2A.

Whilst reservation about the classification was expressed by Lord Nicholls in ***Royal Bank of Scotland Plc v Etridge (No 2) [2001]*** the classes continue to exist although the importance of the division should not be overstated.

An example of actual undue influence:

In the case of ***Williams v Bayley [1866]***, the son of Mr Williams gave a promissory note to the bank upon which he had forged Mr Williams signature. When the bank discovered this, they organised a meeting with Mr Williams. They asked him to pay his son's debts, or they would press charges against the son. Mr Williams agreed to take on a mortgage that allowed him to pay of his son's debts. Later, he sought to have the mortgage put aside. The court held that Mr Williams was allowed to set aside the contract because 'the agreement has been extorted from the father by undue pressure.'

It is clear that the son committed a fraud and therefore the bank had a right to press charges against the son. What the bank should not have done was use the love of the father for his son against the father by putting pressure on the latter to meet his son's debts.

There is a close link between actual undue influence and economic duress, but actual undue influence continues to be a separate course of action.

An example of presumed undue influence:

Allcard v Skinner [1877]: A young woman joined a religious organisation called the Sisters of the Poor. She built up a strong relationship with the pastor and the mother superior. One of the requirements for joining the sisterhood was that she would give up all her personal possessions and she would not seek independent advice without authorisation from the mother superior. In 1879 she left the convent and in 1885 she sought to recover her property.

The court held that there had been undue influence but that she could not reclaim her property because the time lapse had affirmed the contract so it could no longer be rescinded.

It is important to note that the court did not suggest that the mother superior had behaved wrongly: "*No deception was practiced upon her [the plaintiff], no unfair advantage was taken of her, none or her money was obtained or applied for any purpose other than the legitimate objects of the sisterhood."*

However, the young woman was heavily under influence of her religious leaders, had taken decisions that were not in her own benefit, and had not been given any independent advice prior to making the decision. Therefore, the focus of presumed undue influence is more on the position of the victim than on the intentions of the party exercising the influence.

10. What elements are needed for presumed undue influence?

- A relationship of trust and confidence between the parties.
- Something about the transaction must call for an explanation.

If so, there is presumed undue influence. The alleged victim does not need to prove there was undue influence if the above criteria are fulfilled.

The presumption can be rebutted. It must be shown that the contract was the result of the exercise of independent will. The easiest way to prove this is to show that the alleged victim received independent professional advice before entering into the contract. This is not always enough as just because advice was available does not mean the alleged victim was free to act upon it.

11. What do we mean that something about the transaction must call for an explanation?

The transaction should be an unusual one. Earlier cases emphasise that the transaction should be disadvantageous to the alleged victim. However, since ***Royal Bank of Scotland Plc v Etridge (No 2) [2001]*** the standard is that there must be ***something unusual about the transaction***.

Example: Tim is Raphael's pastor. Tim offers to buy Raphael's bike for £300. This is what the bike would be worth if he had sold it to someone else. This is not an unusual transaction. Therefore, the pastoral relationship between Raphael and Tim is not relevant and there is no presumed undue influence.

Now, Tim offers to buy Raphael's house. The house is worth about £300,000 and Tim offers £100,000 for the house which Raphael accepts. The transaction calls for an explanation. There is likely to be presumed undue influence.

In ***Hamond v Osborn [2002]*** an older man (Pritler) gave his carer (Osborn) four cheques for a total value of £297,000. The transactions left him without much money and a big tax bill. When Mr Pritler passed away his family sought to set aside the gifts to the carer. The court held that there had been undue influence because of the size of the transaction, the small amount Mr Pritler had left after the transaction, and the lack of any kind of independent advice for Mr Pritler. The behaviour of Mr Osborn was not relevant: *"even if it is correct to say that Mrs Osborn's conduct was unimpeachable and that there was nothing sinister in it, that would be no answer to an application of the presumption."*

In ***R v Attorney General for England and Wales [2003]*** undue influence was also mentioned. There was no doubt that R was in a relationship of trust and confidence with his superiors but the transaction itself (the confidentiality agreement regarding his time in the SAS) was not seen as unusual.

12. What are three party cases?

These cases arose out of a common scenario. The husband was a business owner of a usually failing business and sought a loan from the bank. The bank agreed to this, but on condition that the husband would put up his house as a guarantee against the loan. As the wife would be a joined owner of the matrimonial home her signature was also needed. The husband would end up not being able to repay the loan and the bank would take possession of the house. The wife would then claim unawareness of what she had signed and would contest the guarantee. It is important to note that the relationship between husband and wife is not a class 2a one but can be a class 2b one if the alleged victim can prove this.

The first case that explored the issue in depth was ***Barclays Bank Plc v O'Brien [1994]***. Mr O'Brien negotiated an overdraft with Barclays regarding his company. Mr O'Brien would guarantee the debts of the company through a charge on his house. He co-owned the house with Mrs O'Brien which meant she needed to sign. She was given no explanation of what she signed or what the consequences could be. The debts of the company rose, and the bank sought repossession of the house. Mrs O'Brien claimed that she had been induced to sign by her husband who had misrepresented the truth to her. The bank stated that whilst this might be the case it was not their responsibility.

The House of Lords held that in such a transaction the bank should be put on notice of the possibility that there might be some wrongdoing on the part of the husband and that the bank had a responsibility to take certain steps to guard against this if:

1) The transaction is not to the financial advantage of the wife.
2) There is a risk of this agreement being obtained by undue influence.

This was followed by the key case of ***Royal Bank of Scotland Plc v Etridge (No 2) [2001]***. This case confirmed that ***the bank is put on inquiry*** whenever a spouse offers to stand guarantee for the debts of their spouse or of their business, and that the bank must ensure that the spouse gets ***independent advice*** before they sign the contract.

Whilst all of these cases were in the context of a married heterosexual couple, this applies to any couple, regardless of gender or marital status or whether or not they live together. Furthermore, it also extends to other non-commercial relationships such as siblings, parents/children, good friends etc. (***Credit Lyonnais Bank Nederland v Burch [1997]***).

The bank is not put on inquiry if the loan is advanced to both parties (because then they would both be part of the loan agreement).

With regards to the other contracting party (the person who is co-signing the guarantee) the bank should take reasonable steps to avoid constructive notice which could entail:

- Have a private meeting with this other party to explain the risks.
- Instead of a private meeting the bank can chose to rely on conformation from a solicitor that independent advice was given to the other party.
- Ensure the other party knows the point of the procedure is that they cannot dispute the transaction later.
- Provide the solicitor with needed financial information.
- Notify the solicitor if there is a suspicion the other party is being misled or not acting freely.

Specific guidelines exist for solicitors as established by Lord Nicholls in ***Royal Bank of Scotland Plc v Etridge (No 2) [2001]***.

The burden of proof that the bank does not have constructive notice is on the bank (***Barclays Bank PLC v Boulter [1997]***).

12. What remedies are there for duress and undue influence?

The contract becomes ***voidable and recission is available***, provided the bars to recission do not apply. If recission is not possible the victim is left without a remedy as contractual damages are not available.

Recission means that the parties are discharged from their obligations and that they are restored to their original positions. The contract remains valid until it is rescinded.

The bars to rescission are:

- *Third party rights* – a third party has acquired a right in the subject matter of the contract
- *Lapse of time (laches)*
- *Affirmation of the contract*

- *Restitution in integrum impossible* – impossibility of precise mutual restoration should not bar rescission and damages could be used to compensate for this.

Duress and undue influence are not a distinctive category of tort and there must therefore be another actionable basis in tort (such as harassment) to make a claim in tort. If there is such an actionable basis damages in tort could be available.

13. What is unconscionability?

In English contract law this is not a well-developed principle, but courts have applied it in extra-ordinary circumstances. It refers to a contract that no person of good conscience would have made and focuses more on substantive unfairness rather than just procedural unfairness. Case law shows a focus on the abuse of naivety (***Earl of Aylesford v Morris [1873]***), abuse of ignorance (***Fry v Lane [1888]***), and the moral impropriety of the contract (***Alec Lobb (Garages) Ltd v Total Oil Ltd [1895]***).

Summary:

There are three kinds of duress:

- duress against the person (oldest form).
- economic duress (still in development).
- duress of goods (contested, in development).

The main conditions for duress are:

- Illegitimate pressure on the alleged victim.
- Lack of a reasonable alternative action.
- Causal link between the pressure and agreement to contract (inducement) – in cases of economic duress: 'But for' test.
- Steps taken by the alleged victim to avoid the contract once this is possible.
- Economic/commercial pressure is not sufficient to prove duress: This is part of normal contract bargaining.

Undue influence was developed in equity as a reaction to the high threshold for duress under the common law.

There are two classes of undue influence:

- Class 1: Actual Undue Influence.
- Class 2a: Presumed Undue Influence arising out of a relationship of trust and confidence in defined categories such as parent-child,

guardian-ward, solicitor-client, religious leader-follower. The presumption can be rebutted.

- Class 2b: Presumed Undue Influence in relationships that do not follow under 2a, but where the alleged victim can prove the relationship gave rise to undue influence.
- Something about the transaction must call for an explanation.
- In three party cases the bank is put on inquiry and must prove that the co-signee of the guarantee knew what they were signing and received independent advice.

Problem Question:

Raven Ltd. concluded a contract with Ships Unlimited to refurbish a ship. The contract stipulates that the ship should be ready in April 2022, before the start of the lucrative summer season. Ships Unlimited has a charter with a holiday company, Cruising Dreams, which begins in May 2022. Cruising Dreams organises cruises in the Mediterranean and the newly refurbished ship will be the star attraction for the season. At the end of March 2022 Raven Ltd contacts Ships Unlimited and asks for an extra payment of £30,000. They explain that if Ships Unlimited does not pay they will not continue to work on the ship and that therefore the ship will not be ready on time. This means that Ships Unlimited will be in breach of contract with Cruising Dreams. Cruising Dreams stands to lose a significant amount of trade because of the late delivery. This is extremely worrying for Ships Unlimited as they likely will be financially responsible, and they have significant cashflow problems already and could go bankrupt if they breach the Cruising Dreams contract. They therefore reluctantly agree to pay the extra money. The ship is delivered on time. Ships Unlimited pays Raven Ltd. the original agreed amount but refuses to pay the extra money.

Advise Raven Ltd. whether they have a remedy

For any change in contract there needs to be consideration. Clearly, Raven Ltd gets the extra £30,000 but it is less clear what the consideration is for Ships Unlimited. They are getting a refurbished ship which they already paid for. In ***Williams v Roffey Bros [1991]*** in a similar situation the other party got a practical benefit out of the situation. Here the practical benefit would get Ships Unlimited their ship on time so they would be able to honour their contract with Cruising Dreams and they would not need to go through the trouble of finding other contractors. Therefore, the variation is supported by consideration.

Ships Unlimited would likely state that they only agreed under duress. This could constitute economic duress as there would be a significant economic pressure upon Ships Unlimited to agree with the contract variation ***(The Sibeon & The Sibotre) [1976]***). Four factors would need to be fulfilled: 1) Was the pressure legitimate? 2) Did the duress induce Ships Unlimited to enter into the contract? 3) Was there a reasonable course of action available for Ships Unlimited? and 4) Did Ships Unlimited take action to avoid the contract?

It should be asked whether the pressure was legitimate (***Universe Tankships v International Transport Workers' Federation (The Universe Sentinel) [1983]***). It is fine to ask for a variation of contract but threatening to breach the contract could be seen as illegitimate (***Atlas Express Ltd v Kafco (Importers & Distributors) Ltd [1989]***).

There clearly would have been significant pressure on Ships Unlimited as a breach of contract by Raven Ltd would have caused economic difficulties for Ships Unlimited as they would not be able to honour their contract with Cruising Dreams.

Would the duress have induced Ships Unlimited to agree to the contractual variation? For economic duress the appropriate test is 'but for' (***Huyton SA v Peter Cremer GmbH & Co [1999]***). Would Ships Unlimited have agreed to the variation in contract if the economic duress had not been present? Would they agreed to the change in contract if they did not have the financial pressure given their cashflow situation and the charter party with Cruising Dreams?

The final question is whether there was a reasonable alternative for Ships Unlimited (***Hoyton SA v Peter Cremer GmbH [1999]***). Given the very limited time between Raven Ltd's demand for extra money and delivery time it would have been difficult/impossible for Ships Unlimited to find another contractor to finish the work in time. This is compounded by the cashflow problems which would make it difficult for Ships Unlimited to engage another contractor as they might ask for a deposit or payment in advance. Ships Unlimited agreed but protested as soon as the duress stopped by not paying the extra amount.

It is therefore likely that the court would find there was economic duress.

Key Cases

Allcard v Skinner [1877 36 Ch D 145]: class 2 A undue influence

Atlas Express Ltd v Kafco (Importers & Distributors) Ltd [1989] 1 All ER 64: threat to break the contract

B&S Contracts and Design Ltd v Victor Green Publications Ltd [1984] ICR 419: importance of lack of a reasonable alternative

BCCI S.A. v. Aboody [1992] 4 All ER 955: actual undue influence
Bank of India v Riat [2014] *EWHC 1775 (Ch):* duress unlikely when concluding a contract
Barclays Bank Plc v O'Brien [1994] *1 AC 180*: bank put on enquiry in undue influence cases
Barton v Armstrong [1976] AC 104: duress of the person
Berntsen v National Westminster Bank [2012]*:* existing liabilities and duress
CIBC Mortgages v Pitt [1994] *1 AC 200*): manifest disadvantage in actual undue influence
Credit Lyonnais Bank Nederland NV v Burch [1997] *1 All ER 144):* responsibility of bank in three party cases not just applicable for spouses, but also in other non-commercial relations.
Dimskal Shipping v ITWF (The Evia Luck) [1991] 4 All ER 871: recognition of duress of goods
Hamond v Osborn & Arnor [2002] EWCA Civ 885: behaviour of the defendant
Hoyton SA v Peter Cremer GmbH [1999] 1 Lloyd's Rep 620: sine qua non in economic duress
Lloyds Bank Ltd v Bundy [1974] *EWCA 8:* class 2 B undue influence
Maskell v Horner [1915] *3 KB 106:* duress of goods in restitution claims
North Ocean Shipping Co v Hyundai Construction Co (The Atlantic Baron) [1979] QB 705: first application of economic duress
Occidental Worldwide Investment v Skibs (The Sibeon & The Sibotre) [1976] 1 Lloyds Rep 293: first recognition of economic duress
Pao On v Lau Yiu Long [1979] 3 All ER 65*:* four factors to prove coercion of the will
R *v Attorney General for England and Wales* [2003] UKPC 22: broadening of duress
Royal Bank of Scotland Plc v Etridge (No 2) [2001] UKHL 44: leading case on undue influence
Skeate v Beale [1841] *11 Ad & E 983:* duress of goods, now outdated but not clearly overruled
Universe Tankships of Monrovia v International Transport Workers' Federation (The Universe Sentinel) [1988] AC 111: considers legitimacy of pressure and absence of choice
Williams v Bayley [1866] LR 1 HL 200: actual undue influence

CHAPTER X

MISREPRESENTATION

Learning Outcomes:

After reading this chapter, you should be able to understand:

- ✓ What statements amount to misrepresentation;
- ✓ The necessary elements for an actionable misrepresentation;
- ✓ The types of misrepresentation;
- ✓ The remedies for misrepresentation.

Questions and Answers:

1. What is misrepresentation?

A representation is a statement made by one of the parties before entering into the contract. The statement would encourage the other party to enter into the contract, but it is not considered a term of the contract (See Chapter VII).

A misrepresentation is a representation that is false. This statement can be made in writing, orally, or through conduct. The contract is not breached because a representation is not a term of the contract. ***A misrepresentation renders the contract voidable***.

A misrepresentation must be:

- Made by one party to the other (or by an agent of the party acting within his authority);
- A statement of existing fact;
- Generally, in the form of a positive statement, rather than silence (exceptions apply);
- At least partly induce the other party to enter into the contract.

To interpret the meaning of a statement the court uses ***the perspective of the reasonable person*** (***Foster v Action Aviation Ltd [2013]***).

There are specific rules for consumer contracts (See the Unfair Trading Practices Act 2008 with regard to misleading actions and misleading omissions).

2. How is inducement decided?

The misrepresentation must be important enough to influence a reasonable person to enter into the contract. It must be material. The representee must have relied on that statement and it must have influenced him to enter into the contract. There is thus a need for both ***materiality and reliance*** (***JEB Fasteners Ltd v Marks Bloom & Co [1983]***).

Warren J in ***Dadourian Group International Inc v Simms [2009]*** summarised inducement:

1. Inducement is a question of fact.
2. If the misrepresentation would likely influence a reasonable person to enter into the contract there is a presumption that it induced the misrepresentee. This presumption is rebuttable.
3. The misrepresentation should play a substantial part in the decision to enter into the contract but does not need to be the sole or decisive part.
4. The presumption is rebutted if the misrepresentor demonstrates that the misrepresentation played no substantial part, but he does not have to show it plays no part.
5. The court decides on inducement on a balance of probabilities.

Courts are not likely to find that there has been an inducement if the misrepresentee:

- Was not aware of the misrepresentation (***Horsfall v Thomas [1862]***).
- Knew before the contract was agreed that the statement was untrue (***JEB Fastener v Marks Bloom & Co [1983]***). However, even if the misrepresentee had serious doubts about the truth of the statement that does not necessarily mean he was not induced by the statement.
- Did not allow the misrepresentation to influence him, even though he was aware of the statement (***Smith v Chadwick [1884]***).
- Relied on his own assessment or on independent advice (***Attwood v Small [1838]***).

A chance to discover the truth does not prevent an actionable misrepresentation. In ***Redgrave v Hurt [1881]*** the seller of a solicitor's firm misrepresented the finances of the firm to the buyer. The true financial position was set out in the accounts which were made available to the buyer to inspect. The buyer did not do so. The court held that there was misrepresentation because the buyer was not obliged to find out whether what the seller said was true. The exception is if the true position is set out in the contract itself (***Peekay Intermark Ltd v Australia and New Zealand Banking Group Ltd [2006]***).

3. What is a statement of fact?

A misrepresentation is ***a statement of fact***. It should be objectively verifiable that the statement is false. In principle statements of mere puff, opinion, intention, and law do not amount to misrepresentation.

A statement of opinion (if genuinely held) does not amount to misrepresentation.

In ***Bisset v Wilkinson [1927]*** a buyer asked the seller of farmland whether the land could support sheep. The seller said that in his opinion the land could support 2,000 sheep. However, this was not the case. The Privy Council held this was a statement of opinion and did not amount to misrepresentation. Parts of the land had never been used for sheep farming; therefore, the opinion of the seller was not based on any real facts.

There are exceptions:

- The opinion must not be contradicted by other facts known to the person giving it.

Example: Smith v Land and House Property Corporation [1884] where a tenant was described by the seller as 'most desirable' even if the tenant had not paid the rent for several months and therefore objectively could not be described as a desirable tenant.

- If the statement comes from an expert in the area it may amount to misrepresentation.

Example: Esso Petroleum Co Ltd v Mardon [1976] where the potential tenant of a petrol station asked the owner how many gallons of petrol he thought could be put through in a year. The owner, who had 40 years of experience, estimated 200,000 to 250,000 gallons a year. In reality the put through of petrol was significantly less (78,000 gallons). The tenant wanted the contract set aside. The court held that there was misrepresentation because the owner had presented himself as an expert, he could have known this was not true, and it was expected that the tenant would rely on that statement.

- If the statement of opinion is not genuinely held it can amount to misrepresentation.

A statement of intention (I will do X or Y) is not a misrepresentation, as long as the intention was genuine at the time of making the statement In ***Edgington v Fitzmaurice [1885]*** a company was in debt and in need of money. They designed a prospectus to attract new investors. The prospectus included information on what the money would be used for: altering the existing buildings, creating more space, and buying horses. In reality, the company already knew they would use the money to pay off their debts.

As the intention stated in the brochure was not genuine, the court held there was misrepresentation. Bowen LJ: *"The state of a man's mind is as much a fact as the state of his digestion. It is true that it is very difficult to prove what the state of a man's mind at a particular time is, but if it can be ascertained it is as much a fact as anything else. A misrepresentation as to the state of a man's mind is therefore a misstatement of fact."*

Statements of law are traditionally not held to be an actionable misrepresentation (***Kleiwort Benson Ltd v Lincoln City Council [1992]***). A statement as to how the law applies to a specific situation can amount to misrepresentation (***Pankhania v Hackney London Borough Council [2002]***).

4. What is meant by 'mere puff'?

Mere puff refers to vague statements and sales talk. These are not considered misrepresentation. This would include statements as: 'this is a once in a lifetime opportunity', 'the food here is the best you will ever have', 'you won't find a better deal within a 100 miles', 'this cleaning products gets even the worst stains out…'

These types of statements are considered to be part of commercial negotiations and/or are too vague to be a cause for action. In ***Dimmock v Hallett [1866]*** a statement was made on how the land was 'fertile and improvable.' This was considered too vague to amount to a representation.

5. Can silence be misrepresentation?

Misrepresentation usually requires ***an active representation***. This can be made orally, in writing, or through conduct.

Spice Girls Ltd v Aprilia World Service BV [2000] is an example of misrepresentation through conduct. The pop group Spice Girls negotiated a contract for the promotion of Aprilia's scooters. They filmed a short commercial just before the contract was signed. All of the promotion materials Aprilia created had the five girls on them. All five girls were present during the negotiations. After the contract was signed Geri Halliwell (Ginger Spice) announced that she was leaving the group. During the negotiations all members already knew that Ginger Spice was planning to leave. They were sued for misrepresentation. During the negotiations it was never said explicitly that all five members would stay in the group and be a part of the promotion campaign. Nonetheless, the court held that their conduct during the negotiations such as the participation of all the girls in the commercial was sufficient to amount to misrepresentation.

Silence in general does not constitute misrepresentation. This is related to the fact that there is no overall pre-contractual duty of good faith in English contract law (which is different from civil law countries). In general, English contract law does not impose a positive obligation to tell everything to the other party, but there is a negative obligation that you are not allowed to lie. In ***Keates v Earl of Cadogan [1851]*** the landlord did not tell the tenant that the property was uninhabitable and as the tenant never asked about the state of the property this was not held to be a misrepresentation.

The exception is ***Uberrim Fidei contracts***, contracts of the utmost good faith. These are contracts where there is fiduciary relationship of trust and confidence such as between a solicitor and a client and the principal and his agent. There is an expectation here that the parties will disclose all facts and if not, this might be considered misrepresentation.

This exception also applies to:

- Insurance contracts (*Lambert v Co-Operative Insurance Society [1975]* (excludes consumer insurance contracts: see Consumer Insurance Act 2012). For insurance contracts: see also Insurance Act 2015).
- Family settlements (*Gordon v Gordon [1816]*).

The law can also impose duties of disclosures through statutory legislation, for instance in relation to financial instruments.

The parties can also include a clause in the contract that imposes a duty of disclosure of certain information.

If defects are deliberately hidden silence can amount to misrepresentation (***Schneider v Heath [1813]***). ***An omission or half-truth*** can be an actionable misrepresentation. In ***Dimmock v Hallett [1966]*** the seller of a block of flats told the buyer that the flats were fully let. Whilst this was true at the time, the seller also knew that the tenants had given notice and were leaving. He omitted to tell the buyer this part. This constituted misrepresentation.

6. What happens if the situation changes?

If there is a representation and the statement is true when it is made, but the situation changes which means the statement is no longer true, there is ***an obligation to notify the representee of the change in circumstances.*** Failure to do so can result in an actionable misrepresentation.

In ***With v O'Flanagan [1936]*** *a* successful medical practice was put on the market and the buyer was told the practice made £2,000 a year. The doctor fell ill and was replaced by a locum and the income of the practice went down significantly (to £5 a week). The buyer was never informed of the change in circumstances and the loss of income before he signed the contract. When he discovered this, he wanted the contract set aside. The court held that there had been a misrepresentation.

A misrepresentation can be continuous if it continues to be relied on and is not withdrawn (***Cramaso LLP v Ogilvie-Grant [2014]***).

7. What are the types of misrepresentation?

- Fraudulent
- Negligent
- Innocent

8. What is fraudulent misrepresentation?

The representation took place 'knowingly or without belief in its truth or recklessly careless whether it be true or false' (Lord Herschell in ***Derry v Peek [1889]***).

If fraud is proven, the motive of misrepresentor is immaterial.

9. What is negligent misrepresentation?

The common law originally only recognised fraudulent and non-fraudulent misrepresentation. Under the common law, action was not possible for non-fraudulent mis misrepresentation.

Hedley Byrne & Co Ltd v Heller & Partners Ltd [1964] recognised that negligent misrepresentation could be actionable if:

- The misrepresentor is in possession of the particular type of knowledge for which advice is required.
- There is sufficient proximity between the two parties so that it is normal to rely on the statement (there is a special or fiduciary relationship).
- The misrepresentee relies on the statement and the misrepresentor is aware of this.
- The burden to prove this is on the misrepresentee.

The law changed with the Misrepresentation Act 1967, Section 2: "*The party who makes a negligent misrepresentation is liable, if he would be liable had the statement been made fraudulently unless he proves that he had reasonable grounds to believe and did believe up to the time that the contract was made that his statement was true."*

There is no need to prove a 'special relationship' or a breach of a duty of care as under ***Hedley Byrne [1964]***. The burden of proving reasonable and factual belief in the truth of statement is on the misrepresentor.

10. What is innocent misrepresentation?

The statement is neither fraudulent nor negligent. The person making the statement would have reasonable grounds to believe that the statement was true.

11. What are the remedies for misrepresentation?

Misrepresentation renders the contract voidable.

Rescission is available for all types of misrepresentation. The bars to rescission apply:

- Affirmation (***Long v Lloyd [1958]***);
- Restoration is not possible; 'restitutio in integrum' but see also: ***Erlanger v New Sombrero Phosphate Co [1878]***);
- Supervening third party rights (***Lewis v Array [1975]***);
- Lapse of time (laches) (***Leaf v International Galleries [1950]***).

Courts should be careful when deciding that there can be no recission because restitution is not possible. If a form of counter-restitution is possible the recission should be allowed (***Salt v Stratstone Specialist Ltd [2015]***).

Rescission can be done through notice or through a court order. In some circumstances this notice can be given to another party than the misrepresentor. For instance, in ***Car & Universal Finance Co v Caldwell [1965]*** notice was given to the police and the AAA because the misrepresentor could not be found.

In case of fraudulent or negligent misrepresentation the time shall be counted from the day of discovery of the misrepresentation.

Damages for fraudulent misrepresentation can be awarded to compensate for all the direct loss the misrepresentee has incurred as a result of the misrepresentation, not merely what was contemplated (reliance measures). Under the common law the measures for damages would be under the tort of deceit (***Doyle v Olly (Ironmongers) Ltd [1969]***). It is also possible to claim for the loss of profit resulting from entering into the contract (***East v Maurer [1991]***).

For negligent misrepresentation the law distinguishes between damages under the common law and damages available under the act.

Damages for negligent misrepresentation under the common law have the object to put the claimant in the position they would have been in had the misrepresentation not occurred. Damages are based on the tort of negligence. The misrepresentee can only recover damages for losses which were reasonably foreseeable by the misrepresentor (and therefore not all direct loss such as for fraudulent misrepresentation).

The rules on remoteness of damages for negligent misrepresentation under Section 2(1) of the Misrepresentation Act 1967 are the same as for fraudulent misrepresentation. Therefore, all direct loss incurred as a result of the statement can be recovered as the wording of the act does not distinguish between the two (***Royscot Trust Ltd v Rogerson [1991]***).

The misrepresentee has a duty to take reasonable steps to mitigate their loss.

The Contributory Negligence Act 1945 does not apply in cases of fraud (***Alliance and Leicester Building Society v Edgestop Ltd [1994]***).

Damages may be awarded under Section 2(2) of the Misrepresentation Act 1967 for non-fraudulent misrepresentation when the contract has been or ought to have been rescinded but the court is of the opinion that it is equitable to award damages instead. This could be for instance if recission would allow the misrepresentee to escape a bad bargain or because it would cause undue hardship on the misrepresentor (***Williams Sindell PLC v Cambridgeshire County Council [1994]***). Damages can only be awarded for innocent misrepresentation if recission is possible, if recission is not available damages can also not be awarded (***Salt v Stratstone Specialist Ltd [2015]***).

Fraud and negligence are easier to prove under Section 2(1) of the Misrepresentation Act 1967 than under the common law. It could still be necessary to sue under the common law, especially for third parties who, because of the lack of a contract, cannot sue under the Act.

Summary:

- A misrepresentation is a false statement of fact made between the parties, that is material, is relied upon, and induces the misrepresentee to enter into the contract.
- For a representation to be an actionable misrepresentation it should be a statement of fact. Mere puff and other vague statements are not a misrepresentation.

- A statement of opinion is not an actionable misrepresentation unless it is made by an expert in the area or if it contradicts existing facts.
- A statement of law is not an actionable misrepresentation, but a false statement as to how the law applies can be.
- A statement of intention is not an actionable misrepresentation unless the statement is not genuinely held.
- Misrepresentation can be made orally, in writing, or through conduct but generally requires an active assertation.
- Half-truths can be a misrepresentation and changes in circumstances should be told to the representee.
- There are three types of misrepresentation:
  - Fraudulent
  - Negligent
  - Innocent
- Remedies include rescission and damages. The key statutory instrument is the Misrepresentation Act 1967.

Problem Question:

Paige is selling a café. Frederick is interested in buying the café. The negotiations take place in January. Paige tells Frederick that the income for the cafe last year was £45,000. She tells Frederick that he can call her accountant if he wants to see the books. She then states that this is the only café in the area and she has no intention of opening a competing café as she is moving to the coast to start a new life. She also tells Frederick that a new campsite is opening in the park which will mean a lot more business for the café. Frederick is very enthusiastic, and he buys the café.

After the contract is concluded in March, Frederick discovers that the income last year was only £25,000. He did not contact the accountant because he did not have time and trusted Paige. To his dismay he also discovers that in February the campsite was refused planning permission by the council and is therefore not opening. Frederick is not sure what to do and things get even worse when Paige's new life plans do not work out and in July, she decides to open a rival café in the area. Frederick now wants to rescind the contract.

Advise Frederick

The first statement Paige makes is that the café made £45,000. This was not true as the accounts proved. It was only £25,000. A misrepresentation is a false statement of fact. Paige did give Frederick a chance to discover the truth but that does not excuse that she made a false statement (***Redgrave v Hurt [1881]***). This could be considered a misrepresentation.

The second statement is a statement of intention. This is in general not an actionable misrepresentation. It would be different if the intention was not genuinely held (***Edgington v Fitzmaurice [1885]***). However, if Paige honestly intended to move further away and then changed her mind this would not be an actionable misrepresentation.

The third statement is more difficult to classify. In principle if there is a change in circumstances the other party should be told about this (***With v O'Flanagan [1936]***). There are several difficulties here: first of all, the change in circumstances concerns an outside event that has nothing to do with Paige. It could very well be that Paige was not aware of this change, and it is questionable whether she had a duty to know this. Secondly, it is not certain this is more than a statement of opinion (***Bisset v Wilkinson [1927]***). Would a campsite in a nearby park really lead to increased business? It could very well be that this statement would be seen as too vague to be an actionable misrepresentation.

Would the first statement have induced Frederick into buying the café? Both materiality and reliance are necessary (***JEB Fasteners Ltd v Marks Bloom & Co [1983]***). The statement is certainly material as it concerns the income of the company, and a reasonable person would be induced by it (***Dadourian Group International Inc v Simms [2009]***). It seems Frederick relied on it, did not seek outside expertise (***Attwood v Small [1838]***), believed Paige, and was aware of the statement (***Horsfall v Thomas [1862]***). Therefore, materiality, reliance, and inducement are present.

Based on this Frederick can likely rescind the contract if none of the bars for rescission apply. Under the Misrepresentation Act 1967 damages for loss would be available if the misrepresentation is judged fraudulent or negligent which seems likely.

Key Cases

Alliance and Leicester Building Society v Edgestop Ltd [1994] 2 ALL ER 28: role of Contributory Negligence Act 1945

Attwood v Small [1838] *UKHL J60*: misrepresentee relied on this own assessment or on independent advice

Bisset v Wilkinson [1927] *AC 177*: statement of opinion

Car & Universal Finance Co v Caldwell [1965] *1 QB 525:* recission through notice to a third party

Cramaso LLP v Ogilvie-Grant [2014] UKSC 9: continuing misrepresentation

Dadourian Group International Inc v Simms [2006] EWCA 399: test regarding inducement.

Derry v Peek [1889] *14 App Cass 337*: fraudulent misrepresentation

Dimmock v Hallett [1866] *LR 2 Ch App 21*: vague statements & half truths

Doyle v Olly (Ironmongers) Ltd [1969] *2 QB 158*: measure for fraudulent damages under the tort of deceit

Edgington v Fitzmaurice [1885] *29 Ch D 459:* statement of intention not genuinely held

Erlanger v New Sombrero Phosphate Co [1878] Co 3 App Cas 1218: 'restitutio in integrum' not possible

Esso Petroleum Co Ltd v Mardon [1976] *EWCA Civ 4*: statement of opinion made by an expert

Foster v Action Aviation Ltd [2013] EWHC 2930 (QB): reasonable person test

Hedley Byrne & Co Ltd v Heller & Partners Ltd [1964] AC 465: negligent misrepresentation under common law

Horsfall v Thomas [1862] *1 H&C 90:* misrepresentee not aware of the misrepresentation

JEB Fasteners Ltd v Marks Bloom & Co [1983] 1 All ER 583: reliance and materiality

Keates v Earl of Cadogan [1851] *10 CB 591:* silence is not misrepresentation

Lambert v Co-Operative Insurance Society [1975] 2 Lloyd's Rep 485: insurance contracts

Leaf v International Galleries [1950] 2 KB 86: laches as bar to recission

Lewis v Array [1975] QB 98: intervening third party rights as a bar to recission

Long v Lloyd [1958] *2 All ER 402:* affirmation bar to recission

Pankhania & Anor v Hackney London Borough Council [2002] *EWHC 2441*: statement of law applied to a specific situation can be misrepresentation

Peekay Intermark Ltd v Australia and New Zealand Banking Group Ltd [2006] EWCA Civ 386: true position set out in the contract

Redgrave v Hurt [1881] *20 Ch D 1*: a chance to discover the truth

Royscot Trust Ltd v Rogerson [1991] *EWCA Civ 12*: rules on remoteness of loss under the Misrepresentation Act 1967 for negligent misrepresentation

Salt v Stratstone Specialist Ltd [2015] EWCA Civ 745: counter-restitution and recission

Smith v Chadwick [1884] *9 App Cas 187:* misrepresentee not influenced

Smith v Land and House Property Corporation [1884] *LR 28 Ch D 7:* statement of opinion contradicting an existing fact

Spice Girls Ltd v Aprilia World Service BV [2002] EWCA Civ 15: misrepresentation through conduct

Williams Sindell PLC v Cambridgeshire County Council [1994] 1WLR 1016: damages instead of recission

With v O'Flanagan [1936] *Ch 575:* change in circumstances

CHAPTER XI

MISTAKE

Learning Outcomes:

After reading this chapter, you should be able to understand:

- ✓ Common mistake, mutual mistake, and unilateral mistake;
- ✓ The effects of mistake;
- ✓ Which mistakes render a contract void;
- ✓ Examples of different types of mistake.

Questions and Answers:

1. What is a mistake?

A mistake is an error that is made by one or both of the parties and which renders the contract void. The facts of the situation are different from what one or both of the parties assumed at the time of contracting and there was no *consensus ad idem* (meeting of the minds). If the party or parties would have been aware of the real state of affairs they would not have entered into the contract. Mistake vitiates the consent because the facts are different from what was envisaged. Whether a mistake was made should be assessed objectively by the court, and the doctrine is applied sparingly. In ***Smith v Hughes [1871]*** Blackburn LJ stated: "*If the parties are not ad idem there is no contract, unless circumstances are such as to preclude one of the parties from denying that he agreed to the terms of the other.*"

There are three categories of mistake:

- Common mistake
- Mutual mistake
- Unilateral mistake

The law on mistake is generally said to be in a state of flux and the boundaries of the doctrine are not always clear.

2. What is the relationship between frustration and common mistake?

Common mistake and frustration (See Chapter XII) are closely related. They both concern a situation where the parties contracted on the basis of a situation that is now significantly different. The key difference between the two is the timing of the event.

Mistake: The facts at the time of contracting are different from what the parties assumed.

Frustration: The facts at the time of contracting are the same from what the parties assumed, but after the contract is concluded the facts change.

Example: Tamera rents a circus tent from Owain. Tamera wants to hold several circus performances in the tent. The tent is destroyed. Therefore, the situation is radically different from what the parties contemplated at the time of contracting. The existence of the tent is necessary for the performance of the contract. Whether the contract is discharged for frustration or rendered void for mistake depends on the timing of the event.

The circus tent is destroyed the day before the contract is concluded and neither Owain nor Tamera knows that the tent has been destroyed and neither party is at fault: the contract can be declared void for mistake.

The circus tent is destroyed the day after the contract is concluded and neither party is at fault: the contract can be discharged because of frustration.

If the event occurs BEFORE the contract is concluded: Mistake

If the event occurs AFTER the contract is concluded: Frustration

Griffith v Brymer [1903]: The defendant hired a room with a good view of the coronation procession of King Edward VII. The king fell ill, and the procession was cancelled. Crucially, the cancellation of the procession happened before the contract was concluded. Neither of the parties were aware of this at the time. The contract was held void for mistake.

This case be contrasted with ***Krell v Henry [1903]*** whereby the facts were similar, and the court held the contract to be frustrated. The big difference between the cases was that in ***Griffith*** the procession was cancelled before the contract was concluded and in ***Krell*** the procession was cancelled after the contract was concluded.

3. What is a common mistake?

Both parties make the same mistake. There is a common assumption about the state of things. The common assumption should be clear from the contract, or from the circumstances and this assumption should be fundamental to the contract (***Triple Seven MSN 27251 Ltd and another company v Azman Air Services Ltd [2018]***). It makes the contract fundamentally different from what the parties had originally assumed.

These mistakes fall in the following categories:

- Mistake as to the existence of the subject matter (res extincta)

Couturier v Hastie [1856]: The buyer and the seller concluded a contract for the sale of corn. At the time of the sale the corn was in transit on a ship between Salonica and London. The parties were not aware the corn had started to rot, and the captain of the ship had sold the corn. Therefore, the corn was not in existence at the time the contract was concluded: The subject matter of the contract did not exist and the court held that the contract was void.

- Mistake as to title/ownership (res sua)

Cooper v Phibbs [1867]: A nephew leased a fishery from his uncle. When the uncle died the nephew renewed the lease with his aunt. The aunt and the nephew were not aware that the uncle had left the fishery to the nephew in his will. Therefore, the nephew was already the owner of the fishery and could not lease this from himself. The contract was void for common mistake.

- Mistake as to quality

Great Peace v Tsavliris [2003]: The defendants agreed to salvage a ship (the Cape Providence). They hired a ship (the Great Peace) to evacuate the crew. They believed the Great Peace was 35 miles away from the Cape Providence. The Great Peace was in fact 400 miles away from the Cape Providence. The defendants wanted the contract declared void for mistake.

Philips MR set out the conditions for mistake:

- There must be a common assumption as to the existence of a certain state of affairs.
- There must be no warranty that this state of affairs exists.
- The non-existence of the state of affairs should not be attributable to the fault of either party.
- The non-existence of the state of affairs must render performance of the contract impossible.
- The state of affairs should be a vital attribute of the consideration to be provided or of the circumstances that make the contract possible.

The court held that in the above case the conditions were not met. This was a mistake as to the quality of the contract (the distance of the ship to the wreckage) and performance of the contract was still possible.

4. What if the parties have contractually allocated the risk?

The parties could allocate the risk in the contract, either expressly through a clause in the contract or implied. If one of the parties makes a clear promise as to the existence of a certain state of things the contract will not be declared void for mistake. ***The party making the assertation bears the risk if the situation is different than promised.***

In ***McRae v Commonwealth Disposal Commission [1951]*** the defendant sold the wreck of an oil tanker to the plaintiff. The oil tanker was supposed to be located on a reef off the coast of New Guinea. The buyer made salvage arrangements and discovered that the tanker did not exist, nor had it ever existed. He sued for breach of contract. The court held that there was no mistake because the seller had clearly affirmed that the oil tanker existed. The existence of the tanker was an implied term of the contract.

5. What is a mistake of quality?

Bell v Lever Bros Ltd [1931] is a key case regarding mistake of quality. Mr Bell and Mr Snelling were the employees of a company called Lever Bros. They breached their contract because they speculated on cocoa prices which their employment contract forbade. The two employees agreed to redundancy in return for a sum of money. After payment Lever Bros discovered that the company was entitled to dismiss the employees without compensation. They sued to get the compensation sum back. This was a common mistake as to the terms of the employment contract. However, the court held that this mistake was not sufficiently fundamental and concerned the quality of the employment contract and not the subject matter of the contract.

Lord Atkin stated: *"Mistake at to quality of the thing contracted for ...will not affect assent unless it is the mistake of both parties and is as to the existence of some quality which makes the thing without the quality essentially different from the thing as it was believed to be."*

In ***Leaf v International Galleries [1950]***, Ernest Louis bought a painting from International Galleries. He and the seller both thought that the painting was 'Salisbury Cathedral' by John Constable. The buyer later discovered that the painting was not by Constable. The court held that there was a mistake as to the quality but not a mistake on the subject matter of the contract. The subject matter was a painting of Salisbury Cathedral which the buyer got. The contract was not void.

A contract can be declared void because of mistake of quality if the quality is essential to the contract. In ***Bell v Lever Bros [1931]*** Lord Atkin gave the famous example of a racehorse versus a carthorse. Whilst both are horses, they cannot be used for the same purpose. Therefore, the quality of the horse would be essential to the contract as a racehorse is useless in front of a cart and a carthorse would be useless as a racehorse.

In ***Solle v Butcher [1950]*** Lord Denning held that a contract could be declared voidable for mistake as to quality in equity. He stated that ***Bell v Lever Bros Ltd*** only applied to the common law. ***Great Peace v Tsavliris [2003]*** ended this approach by stating that the House of Lords had made a complete statement as to the law in ***Bell v Lever Bros Ltd.*** This helped to establish further certainty in the law on mistake.

6. What is a mutual mistake?

A mutual mistake means that both parties have made a mistake. However, they have both made a different mistake. They are at cross purposes.

Raffles v Wichelhaus [1864]: Two parties concluded a contract to buy cotton. The cotton would be shipped from India to London on a ship named *Peerless.* There were however two ships named *Peerless* and both would sail from Mumbai to London. One would sail in October and the other in December. The parties both had a different *Peerless* in mind. The parties were thus mistaken about which ship the contract referred to. They both made a mistake, but it was not the same mistake. It was impossible to assess objectively which ship the contract referred to. There was latent ambiguity as to what the parties meant.

7. What is a unilateral mistake?

Only one of the parties made the mistake, but the other party is aware that they made this mistake.

These are mistakes in relation to:

- Terms of the contract
- Identity

Hartog v Colin & Shields [1939] concerned a ***mistake as to the terms of the contract.*** A contract was concluded for the sale of hare skins. The price per pound was 3 times lower than per piece. The negotiations made it clear that the sale was to be per piece as was also the custom in the trade. The final offer contained a mistake and put the price per pound. The buyer was aware that the seller made an error in the final offer.

In ***Shogun Finance v Hudson [2003]***, Lord Philips said: "*If the offeree knows that the offeror does not intend the terms of the offer to be these that the natural meaning of the words would suggest he cannot, by purporting to accept the offer, bind the offeree to the* *contract.*" It is on the mistaken party to prove that the other party was aware of the mistake.

8. What is a mistake as to identity?

This is a unilateral mistake. A concludes a contract with B, but believes that B is C.

In those cases, a rogue often represents himself as being someone else. The contract is voidable for fraudulent misrepresentation. This means that the contract can be rescinded. If the rogue sells the goods to a third party before the contract is rescinded the third party will have obtained good title to the goods. The goods were in the lawful possession of the rogue and are now in the lawful position of the third party. The original seller can sue the rogue and obtain damages for misrepresentation. However, it might be that the rogue cannot be found or even if he is found it might be difficult to obtain damages.

If the contract is declared void because of mistake, the rogue never acquired good title to the goods because the contract never existed. When the rogue sold the goods on to the third party, he had no legal right to do so: ***Nemo dat quod non habet*** (no-one gives what they do not have). This means that the seller can get the goods back. It is up to the third party to sue the rogue to get any damages for his losses.

Therefore, it is often preferable for the original seller to have the contract declared void for mistake rather than voidable for misrepresentation.

A distinction should be made between contracts that were made ***inter absentes*** (where the parties never found themselves face to face) or contracts that the parties concluded ***in each other's presence*** (face to face).

Cundy v Lindsay [1878] concerned a contract concluded *inter absentes*. Lindsay sold handkerchiefs to a rogue named Blenkarn. Blenkarn sold the goods onto other people, including Cundy. Lindsay then sued Cundy under the tort of conversion, arguing that the rogue never had good title to the goods. Blenkarn had signed all his letters Blenkiron & Son with an address in Wood Street. Blenkiron & Son were a well-known business which was indeed located in Wood Street. Lindsay addressed all returning correspondence to Blenkiron & Son. Lindsay therefore argued that he had only intended to do business with Blenkiron & Son. The House of Lords agreed with Lindsay and the contract was declared void because of mistaken identity.

An example of a mistaken identity in a face-to-face contract is ***Philips v Brooks Ltd [1919]***. Mr North bought some jewellery. He stated that his name was Sir George Bullough and gave an address. There was indeed at Sir George Bullough living at that address and he got credit. Mr North resold the jewellery to the defendant. The court held that the plaintiff had intended to contract with the man in his presence which made the contract voidable for fraud but not void for mistake. The seller was mistaken about the credit worthiness of the rogue. He would have sold to anyone entering the shop.

There is a presumption in face-to-face contracts that the parties intend to contract with the person in front of them. The presumption can be rebutted (***Ingram v Little [1961]***). The distinction between face-to-face contracts and contracts in absentia has been criticised as being artificial. Furthermore, the consistency of the caselaw is also criticised whereby very similar facts can lead to different decisions (such as in ***Philips v Brooks Ltd [1919]*** and ***Ingram v Little [1961]***). Nevertheless, the distinction continues to exist

In ***Shogun Finance Ltd v Hudson [2003]*** a rogue impersonated Mr Patel and bought a car on hire-purchase basis. The rogue showed Mr Patel's driver's licence which he had found on the street. The seller passed the information to the finance company who authorised the agreement. The Rogue then sold the car to Mr Hudson. Shogun Finance sought to have the contract declared void so the car would be returned to them.

The court held that there was never a contract between Shogun Finance and the rogue and that therefore the contract was void and Mr Hudson never owned the car. Mr Hudson bought the car in good faith. He now lost the car. He could of course sue the rogue to get his money back, but the rogue had disappeared. Therefore, Mr Hudson due to no fault of his own was now out of pocket.

Mistaken identity has to be about the identity of the person and not about the attributes of a person such as their creditworthiness. The identity has to be fundamental to the contract.

9. Can a contract be rectified?

In exceptional circumstances ***the court can rectify a contract in equity***. The parties were in complete agreement as to the terms of the contract. They made ***an error when they wrote down the terms.***

The scope for this is limited. Peter Gibson LJ stated in ***Swainland Builders Ltd v Freehold Properties Ltd [2002]***:

1. There needs to be a common intention between the parties regarding the issue.

2. This intention should be continuous to the time the agreement was drafted.
3. The agreement does not reflect this common intention.

10. What are the consequences of mistake?

Mistake renders the contract void. The contract is treated as if it never existed.

Summary:

- Mistake means that the facts of the situation are fundamentally different from what the party or the parties assumed at the time of contracting.
- Mistake renders the contract void.
- Mistake as to quality does not render the contract void for mistake unless the quality is fundamental to the contract.

- There are three types of mistakes:

  - Common mistake
  - Mutual mistake
  - Unilateral mistake

- Common mistake: Both parties make the same mistake.

  - Res extincta (the subject matter does not exist).
  - Res sua (mistake as to the title of the goods).

- Mutual mistake: Both parties make a mistake, but it is not the same one.
- Unilateral Mistake: Only one of the parties makes a mistake, but the other party is aware of this.

  - Mistake as to identity.
  - Mistake as to terms of the contract.

Problem Question:

Valeria, who owns a furniture shop, visits Rahiya, one of her suppliers. Valeria spots a beautiful chair that she believes to be a design of top furniture designer Gregor Y. Rahiya and Valeria chat about the chair, Rahiya also thinks the chair is by Gregor Y. Valeria is very happy and decides to buy the chair. They agree on £2,000 for the chair which is a real bargain for a chair by Gregor Y. As Valeria does not have her van with her, she promises to come by tomorrow to pick the chair up. On her way out, Valeria spots a nice table, and she decides to buy that too. She lets Rahiya know of her intention to buy the table and Rahiya promises to set it aside in the warehouse until tomorrow when Valeria returns. That night there is a fire in the warehouse which destroys the table. Rahiya is not aware of this.

The next day Valeria returns to with her van. She takes the chair and negotiates with Rahiya for the table. They conclude the contract for £500 and Rahiya gives Valeria a receipt with which she can go to the warehouse and pick up the table. When Valeria arrives at the warehouse, she is told that the table was destroyed in the fire the previous night.

Even worse is that Valeria finds out that the chair is not designed by Gregor Y but by an unknown designer. The chair is probably worth around £300.

Advise Valeria whether the contracts can be set aside for mistake

The first contract was for the sale of a chair. This is what Valeria got. However, the chair is worth far less than she anticipated because it is not a design chair. From the scenario it seems that both Rahiya and Valeria believed the chair was by Gregor Y. This would be a common mistake. Neither party was at fault and they both made the same assumption.

Rahiya does not seem to have assumed the risk for the mistake as she has not affirmed that the chair was designed by Gregor Y (***McRae v Commonwealth Disposal Commission [1951]***). If they have a written contract which states that the sold object is designed by Gregor Y, Valeria could have a recourse for breach of contract.

The subject matter of the contract is a chair. According to ***Bell v Lever Bros Ltd [1931]*** the contract is still valid even if there is a mistake of quality unless the quality is seen as fundamental to the contract. This case is comparable to ***Leaf v International Galleries [1950]***. The subject matter of the contract is a painting of Salisbury Cathedral. The mistake was as to quality: It was not painted by John Constable but by someone else. It could be said here that Valeria was buying a chair which she got. Of course, Valeria might not have bought the chair if she thought it was not designed by Gregor Y and she certainly would not have paid as much money. Nevertheless, the mistake is likely not fundamental to the contract.

It could be possible to argue that this is a case of innocent misrepresentation which makes the contract voidable. (***Leaf v International Galleries [1950]***) but likely the contract could not be declared void for mistake.

The second transaction is for the table. Valeria spots the table and affirms her intention of buying it, Rahiya agrees to this. Is this enough to form a contract? If the contract is formed at that stage, it would be hard to have the contract set aside for mistake although it might be possible to claim frustration which would discharge the contract (***Taylor v Caldwell [1863]***). However, based on the facts it does not seem as if a contract was concluded. The parties had not made any decisions regarding some key points to the contract (***Scammell v Ouston [1941]***). There was no real offer and acceptance at this point.

This means the contract was concluded the next day. The table was no longer in existence at this point. Both parties believed the table was still in existence. This would be a common mistake. Rahiya does not seem to have affirmed the existence of the table (***McRae v Commonwealth Disposal Commission [1951]***). It was not the fault of either party. This contract could thus be declared void for mistake on the existence of the subject matter: res extincta (***Couturier v Hastie [1856]***).

Key Cases

Bell v Lever Bros Ltd [1931] UKHL 2: common mistake as to quality
Cooper v Phibbs [1867] LR2 HL: mistake as tot title/ownership
Couturier v Hastie [1856] UKHL J3: mistake as to the existence of the subject matter
Cundy v Lindsay [1878] *3 App Case* 459: contract void for mistaken identity
Frederick E Rose (London) Ltd v William H Pin Jnr & Co [1953] 2 QB 450: rectification
Great Peace Shipping v Tsavliris International [2003] QB 679: key modern case on mistake
Griffith v Brymer [1903] 19 TLR 434: event should occur before conclusion of the contract
Hartog v Colin & Shields [1939] *3 All ER 56*: unilateral mistake as to the terms of contract
Ingram v Little [1961] 1 QB 31: rebuttal of presumption in face-to-face contracts
King's Norton Metal Co Ltd v Edridge [1879] 14 TLR 98: attributes of the person
Leaf v International Galleries [1950] 2 KB 86: common mistake as to quality
McRae v Commonwealth Disposal Commission [1951] 84 CLR 377: assumption of risk
Philips v Brooks Ltd [1919] 2 KB 243: mistaken identity in face-to-face contracts
Raffles v Wichelhaus [1864] EWHC Exch J19: mutual mistake
Shogun Finance v Hudson [2003] *UKHL 62*: mistaken identity and documentation
Smith v Hughes [1871] *LR 6 QB 597*: narrow scope of mistake
Solle v Butcher [1950]: contract voidable for common mistake in equity
Swainland Builders Ltd v Freehold Properties Ltd [2002] 2 EGLR: when terms can be rectified
Triple Seven MSN 27251 Ltd and another company v Azman Air Services Ltd [2018] EWHC 1348: mistake should be fundamental to the contract

CHAPTER XII

FRUSTRATION

Learning Outcomes:

After reading this chapter, you should be able to understand:

- ✓ The situations in which the doctrine of frustration applies;
- ✓ The difference between frustration and force majeure;
- ✓ The consequences of frustration;
- ✓ The role of the Law Reform (Frustrated Contracts) Act 1943.

Questions and Answers:

1. What do we mean when a contract is frustrated?

Frustration operates to discharge a contract where, after conclusion, there ***is a significant change of circumstances which renders performance of the contract impossible, illegal, or where the purpose is now radically different from what the parties intended at the time of concluding the contract.*** The contract is discharged from the moment the frustrating event occurs, everything that happened before the event remains valid.

Frustrating events are:

- Impossibility
- Illegality
- Frustration of purpose

Hardship does not frustrate the contract.

2. How did the doctrine of frustration develop?

Common law is strict regarding the performance of contractual obligations. Historically, a party could not be released from their obligations even if the circumstances changed drastically.

In the classic case ***Paradine v Jane [1647]*** a tenant was disposed of his farm for two years because the territory where he is farm was located was occupied by the King's enemies. Even though he could not access the farm he was held liable to pay rent for the entire period: *"though the land be surrounded, or gained by the sea, or made barren by wildfire, the lessor shall have his whole rent."*

Although strict, the law was not absolute. Death could absolve a party from contractual obligations in case of employment contracts and apprenticeships for instance.

A major development in frustration was the key case of ***Taylor v Caldwell [1863]***. The plaintiffs hired Surrey Gardens and Music Hall for 4 non-consecutive days between June and August 1861 for the purpose of holding concerts and fêtes. After the contract was concluded but before the day of the first concert a fire destroyed the music hall. Under ***Paradine v Jane*** the failure to provide the music hall would be considered a breach of contract and would have entitled the plaintiffs to significant damages.

The court however took a different decision. Blackburn J held that "*from the nature of the contract, it appears that the parties must... have known that it could not be fulfilled unless... some particular specified thing continued to exist.*" The existence of the music hall was essential for the contract. There was an implied condition in the contract that the parties would be released from their contractual obligations when performance is impossible.

The law developed further with ***Davis Contractors Ltd v Fareham Urban District Council [1956]***. Davis Contractors submitted a tender for a building scheme to Fareham Urban District Council. The tender was successful, and Davis contracted to build 78 houses within 8 months for £94,425. The work eventually took 22 months because there was a shortage of labourers, and this cost Davis an extra £21,000. Davis argued that the shortage of labourers had frustrated the contract. The court held that there had been no frustration because the cause of delay was foreseeable as there was an all-around shortage of labourers of which Davis was aware as noted in the tender documents.

The court rejected implied condition as the basis for frustration because the parties could have no intentions regarding an unforeseen event. They favoured the approach of ***construction of contractual terms and whether there was a radical difference in how the contract would be performed from what the parties had initially agreed*: *Non haec in foedera veni*** (It was not this that I promised to do).

In the ***Sea Angel [2007]*** Rix LJ said: "*The test of 'radically different' is important; it tells us that the doctrine is not to be lightly invoked; that mere incidence of expense or delay or onerousness is not sufficient; and that there has to be as it were a break in identity between the contract as provided for and contemplated and its performance in the new circumstances.*" ***Whilst radically different is the key principle on which frustration is based, some cases still refer to implied condition as a basis for frustration.***

In English contract law it is not possible for the court to adjust the contract because of a frustrating event. It can only discharge the contract. The court adjusting the contract is possible in some civil law jurisdictions and in transnational commercial law doctrine as evidenced by the UNIDROIT Principles of International Commercial Contracts (Article 6.2.3).

3. When does the doctrine of frustration not apply?

1. When the parties have made provisions for the change in circumstances through for instance a force majeure or hardship clause;
2. When the changed circumstances were foreseeable;
3. When it is the party's own fault that the change in circumstances happened;
4. When a party merely wants to escape a bad bargain.

4. What role does the contract play in establishing whether there is frustration?

When frustration is alleged, the first step for the Court is to look at the contract:

1. To determine the parties' obligations under the contract;
2. To determine whether the contract makes provisions for the changed circumstances (for instance, through a force majeure clause);
3. If the contract does not make any such provisions the doctrine of frustration could apply provided that the conditions for frustration are met: The event was not foreseeable, it makes performance radically different/impossible/illegal, and it was not self-induced.

A temporary frustration can also discharge the contract (***Robinson v Davison [1871]***).

5. What is force majeure?

Force majeure is a term used to indicate that an event has occurred which impedes the performance of the contract. It closely resembles frustration but is usually interpreted more broadly.

In English contract law ***force majeure is introduced through a clause in the contract***. These are clauses which indicate what should happen in the case of a specific event occurring. It usually provides that the contract can be suspended or terminated if those events occur. These events include for instance acts of God, war, terrorism, piratry, industrial action, boycotts, pandemics etc.

6. How can the parties provide for contingencies?

The parties can include different clauses in the contract that provide for what should happen in specific circumstances. This includes force majeure clauses.

A hardship clause provides for what should happen if the contract becomes significantly more onerous to perform. For instance, the parties have concluded a contract for the sale of grain. After conclusion but before performance the harvest fails and the price of grain skyrockets. The contract is now significantly more onerous for the seller who has to source the grain at much higher prices. The seller is not entitled to any adjustments. However, if the parties have included a hardship clause that provides for what should happen in these circumstances (for instance, adjustment of the price or renegotiations) the seller is entitled to the remedy the clause provides.

This includes other type clauses such as ***price adjustment clauses, handcuffs clauses, and delay clauses.*** The court will construe the clause to ascertain whether it covers the particular occurrence.

On construction of the contract the court could find that one of the parties has assumed the risk for the frustrating event such as in ***Dany Lions Car v Bristol Cars [2010]*** where the defendant assured that he would achieve a specific result, even though that result proved to be impossible to achieve.

If the meaning of the clause is not clear the court will construct and interpret the clause. ***Metropolitan Water Board v Dick, Kerr and Co Ltd [1918]*** concerned the construction of a reservoir. The contract contained a delay clause. World War I broke out and the contractors were forced to sell all of their equipment to the government. The court constructed the clause as covering only temporary delays and not such a fundamental change in circumstances. Therefore, the contract was frustrated.

7. When is an event foreseeable?

An event should be unforeseeable otherwise there is no frustration. The difficulty can be to ***identify precisely whether an event is foreseeable*** or not. For instance, is it foreseeable that an earthquake in California would happen? In general California is prone to earthquakes so that does not make it unlikely an earthquake would happen. However, if you conclude a contract for renting a building in California should you expect an earthquake to happen that makes the building inhabitable? Is this a foreseeable event?

In ***Ocean Tramp Tankers v V/O Sovfratcht (The Eugenia) [1964]*** the defendants chartered the ship 'Eugenia' for a voyage to India. The parties discussed whether the voyage should go via the Suez Canal. This would save a considerable amount of time as opposed to sailing past the Cape of Good Hope, but there were also military tensions in Egypt and a real possibility the Suez Canal would close. The parties agreed that the defendants would not enter a zone which was 'dangerous as a result of any actual or threatened act of war.' The Eugenia went via the Suez Canal and entered an area where Egyptian anti-aircraft guns were firing. The ship was trapped for more than 2 months, and the charterers claimed frustration.

The Court held that it was the charterers' fault that they were trapped in the Suez Canal because the parties made provisions in their contract regarding entering dangerous zones. Given the existing military tensions it was foreseeable that this could be a dangerous zone.

Rix LJ held in the ***Sea Angel [2007]*** that *"most events are to a greater or lesser degree foreseeable. That does not mean they cannot lead to frustration."* ***Foreseeability is therefore not absolute but a matter of degree.***

8. What is self-induced frustration?

If the party is responsible for the frustrating event, they cannot rely on the doctrine to escape their contractual obligations.

The Super Servant Two [1990] concerned a contract to carry a rig from Japan to Rotterdam. The contract stipulated two ships that could be used for this purpose: The Super Servant One and Super Servant Two. The defendants decided to use SS2 and to use SS1 for another contract. The SS2 ran into problems at sea and sank. The SS1 being otherwise engaged could not be used and the contract could not be performed. The defendants claimed the contract had been frustrated because the ship sank. The Court held that the contract was not frustrated because the defendants had a choice of ships they could use for this contract, and it was their decision to use the SS1 for another contract. Therefore, the defendants induced the frustrating event.

In ***Maritime National Fish Ltd v Ocean Trawlers Ltd [1935]*** the defendants chartered a ship with an otter trawl (the Saint Cuthbert). To go fishing with an otter trawl they needed a licence. They applied for five licences, but only got three. They decided to use the licences for three of their own ships and not for the chartered ship. They wanted the charter party declared frustrated. The court held that the contract was not frustrated because the charterers could have gotten an otter trawl licence for the Saint Cuthbert, but they had elected not to do so, and to instead nominate their own ships for the licence.

9. When is the contract impossible to perform?

This can be because ***the subject matter of the contract is destroyed*** such as in ***Taylor v Cadwell [1863]***. Section 7 of the Sale of Goods Act 1979 states that the contract is frustrated if goods are destroyed before risk passes and the destruction is not the fault of either party. ***This only applies to sale for specific goods and not sale by description***. In that case, the burden is on the seller to source alternative goods.

In ***Blackburn Bobbing v TW Albert [1918]***, a contract was concluded for the sale of Finnish timber. The seller always got his timber when an order came in and did not stockpile anything. Because of the outbreak of WWI, it became impossible to import the timber from Finland and the seller wanted the contract to be discharged for frustration. The court held that the contract was not frustrated because the timber could be sourced elsewhere (even though that would be more expensive for the seller) and the buyer would not have been aware that it was custom in the industry not to keep any stockpiles of timber. Because this was a known custom it could be that the outcome of the case would have been different if the buyer was a fellow Finnish timber merchant who would have been aware of the custom.

This is different if the contract ***requires the product to be sourced from a specific location*** (***Howell v Coupland [1876]***). In that case the contract could be frustrated if the source is not accessible.

Frustration can also be because of ***the impossibility of the 'adventure'*** (***Jackson v Union Maine Insurance Co Ltd [1874]***). For instance, if a ship is chartered to make a journey at a specific time of the year and the ship is delayed because of a frustrating event the adventure is no longer possible (because it was supposed to occur in a specific period). Impossibility of adventure is often linked with delays.

10. What do we mean with frustration of purpose?

The parties had a specific purpose in mind when they contracted but because of an unforeseen event the purpose can no longer be fulfilled.

A classic example is the so-called 'coronation cases.' The coronation of King Edward VII was to be accompanied by a procession through the streets where people could see the King. Some entrepreneurial people who lived along the route rented out rooms with a view of the procession. Unfortunately, the King fell ill, and the procession had to be cancelled.

In ***Krell v Henry [1903]***, Krell owned an apartment overlooking the route of the procession which he had rented to Henry. Henry had paid the deposit but when the procession was cancelled, he refused to pay the rest. Krell's argument was that whilst the procession was cancelled the rooms could still be used and Henry was welcome to use the rooms that day just as they had contracted for. Henry's argument was that whilst this was true the only reason, he wanted those rooms was to see the procession.

The court held that the rooms were let for a particular purpose which was the foundation of the contract: The coronation procession. Both parties were aware of that purpose. The purpose was frustrated by an unforeseen event. The court made a comparison with hiring a cab to go to Epsom on Derby Day at an enhanced price. If the Derby is cancelled, the cab contract would not be frustrated because the purpose of the contract was to take the person to Epsom and not to take the person to the Derby. It could be argued that the enhanced price would likely be because the cabdriver was aware of the Derby happening. It remains unclear what impact that has on the foundation of the contract.

Krell v Henry [1903] can be contrasted with ***Herne Bay Steamboat v Hutton [1903]***. As part of the coronation events there would be a Royal Naval Review. This was cancelled along with the procession. Hutton hired a ship for the purpose of a day's cruise around the fleet and to see the Royal Naval Review. When the latter was cancelled, Hutton refused to take the ship and pay the balance. The court held that there was no frustration because the Royal Naval Review was not the sole purpose of the contract. The cruise could still take place and the fleet could still be seen. The Royal Naval Review was not held to be the foundation of the contract.

Another important difference was that in ***Krell v Henry***, Krell would have never rented out the rooms if it had not been for the procession, whilst Herne Bay Steamboat always rented out their ships. If Mr Hutton had not chartered the ship from them for the day, they would likely have found another customer regardless of the coronation happening. Krell never rented out his rooms and in the absence of the procession would not have found another customer.

It should be noted that the courts have only applied frustration of purpose in a very small number of cases.

11. How does illegality frustrates the contract?

When the contract was concluded it was legal. However, ***an unforeseeable event has caused the contract to now be illegal. Fibrosa Spolka Akcyjna v Fairbarn Lawson Comber Barbour Ltd [1942]*** concerned a contract to manufacture and deliver certain machines to Poland. When the Nazis invaded Poland, it became illegal for UK companies to trade with Poland. The contract was deemed frustrated.

Illegality refers to ***policy and law changes from any level of government***, including municipal governments and includes changes in zoning, trading hours, and type of events that can be held in a certain location (***Gamenco v ICM Fair Weather Agency [1995]***).

12. What are the effects of frustration?

Frustration kills the contract. The contract is discharged immediately. ***Both parties are released from their obligation to perform the contract from the date of discharge.*** There is no retrospective effect.

Before the introduction of the 1943 Law Reform (Frustrated Contracts) Act it was difficult to recuperate any monies already paid: 'the loss lies where it falls.' There were some exceptions, such as the recovery of a deposit under the law of restitution. In ***Chandler v Webster [1904]*** the Court held that a sum paid in advance could not be recovered and that furthermore as the balance was due before the frustrating event this should also be paid.

This was challenged by ***Fibrosa Spolka Akcyjna v Fairbarn Lawson Comber Barbour Ltd [1942]*** where the court held that if there had been ***a total failure of consideration any deposits or advances paid could be recovered.***

This was still an unsatisfying solution because other monies paid such as expenses could not be recovered and there was no set-off for performed service.

This led to the introduction of the Law Reform (Frustrated Contracts) Act 1943. Section 1(2) states that all sums paid or payable to any party in pursuance of the contract before the time of frustration shall, in the case of sums so paid, be recoverable, and in the case of sums so payable, cease to be payable. This sum shall not exceed the sum payable under the contract and the amount of expenses incurred.

The court may order the recovery of expenses paid. This could be all of the expenses or part of them.

Section 1(3) states that were a party has obtained a valuable benefit (other than money) under the contract before the contract became frustrated the Court may order the value of the said benefit to be recovered where it is just to do so. The recoverable sum shall not exceed the value of the benefit. The Court should consider the expenses incurred by the party who received the benefit and the circumstances that caused the frustration.

It is important to note that ***any monies that can be recovered are at the discretion of the court:*** *"No indication in the Act, the authorities or the relevant literature that the court is obliged to incline towards total retention or equal division. Its task is to do justice in a situation which the parties had neither contemplated nor provided for, and to mitigate the possible harshness of allowing all loss to lie where it has fallen."* (***Gamerco SA v ICM/Fair Warning (Agency) Ltd [1995]***).

The act does not apply to voyage charters, carriage of goods by sea contracts, insurance contracts, and sale of some specific goods.

The court in ***BP Exploration v Hunt [1983]*** held that there are two stages to establish the sum involved under Section 1(3):

1) The identification and valuation of the non-monetary benefit. This is the objective market value.

2) The awarding of a just sum (for which the basis is a 'reasonable value' for the service and the maximum is the valuation established in stage 1).

The court stated that the goal of the Act is not to put the parties in the position they would have been if the contract had been performed nor to divide the loss between the parties

Whilst the 1943 Act made it significantly easier for the parties to recuperate any advances or receive money for services rendered, it does not cover all losses and expenditure. A frustrating event can still lead to one of the parties being significantly out of pocket. Whilst this can seem unfair, it is understandable given the nature of frustration: the event was unforeseeable and was not the fault of either party.

Summary:

- A frustrating event occurs after the contract is formed.
- It renders performance impossible, illegal, or radically different from what was intended (frustration of purpose).
- It should not be foreseeable or self-induced.
- The effect of frustration is that the contract is discharged with immediate effect.
- Under the 1943 Law Reform (Frustrated Contracts) Act it is possible to recuperate any advances and deposits paid. It may also be possible at the discretion of the court to recuperate expenses and the value of benefits obtained.

Problem Question:

Killian concludes a contract with Zephyr to build a stable for £30,000. Zephyr has calculated that the costs of the materials will be around £15,000, labour and other costs £10,000, leaving £5,000 in profits. Zephyr always gets his materials from a specific country where they are very cheap. Unfortunately, because of international tensions Zephyr cannot import from his usual place and has to source the materials elsewhere. Thus, this will cost him around £21,000. This makes the project very expensive, and Zephyr wants to have the contract cancelled because of frustration.

Advise Zephyr

Whilst the contract has become much more expensive for Zephyr to such a point that he is going to lose money on this the contract is likely not frustrated. Frustration does not occur just because the contract is now more onerous to perform. The contract cannot be said to be radically different (***The Sea Angel [2007]***) from what the parties contemplated.

If Zephyr and Killian have included a hardship or price adjustment clause then Killian might have to renegotiate or get the price adjusted.

However, in absence of contractual provisions the contract is likely not frustrated. Whilst the international tensions might not have been foreseeable, the materials can be sourced from elsewhere (***Blackburn Bobbin Co Ltd v T W Allen & Sons Ltd [1918]***). If Killian and Zephyr included in their contract that the materials can be sourced from only this specific country the contract might be frustrated (***Howell v Coupland [1876]***).

The purpose of the contract (making money) might be frustrated for Zephyr, but that is likely not what the court would see as the foundation of the contract (***Krell v Henry [1903]***). The foundation would be building the stable. This purpose has not been frustrated.

- When the building is almost finished Killian discovers that he needed to have planning permission which he does not have. Planning permission is denied. Killian now wants to cancel the contract because of frustration.

Advise Killian

The contract could be seen as frustrated because of illegality (***Fibrosa Spolka Akcyjna v Fairbarn Lawson Comber Barbour Ltd [1942]***). However, Killian is clearly at fault because he did not ask for planning permission. This amounts to self-induced frustration (***The Super Servant Two) [1990]***) and the contract will thus not be discharged for frustration.

Key Cases

Blackburn Bobbin Co Ltd v T W Allen & Sons Ltd [1918] *2 KB 46*: goods by description
BP Exploration Co (Libya) v Hunt (No 2) [1983] *2 AC 352*: stages under Section 1(3) of the Law Reform (Frustrated Contracts) Act 1943
Chandler v Webster [1904] 1 KB 493: the loss lies where it falls
Dany Lions Car v Bristol Cars [2010] *EWHC 2997 (QB):* assumption of risk for frustrating event
Davis Contractors Ltd v Fareham Urban District Council [1956] AC 696: foreseeability
Edwinton Commercial Corporation and Another v Tsavliris Russ (Worldwide Salvage & Towage) Ltd (The Sea Angel) [2007] EWCA Civ 547: the test of 'radically different'
Fibrosa Spolka Akcyjna v Fairbarn Lawson Comber Barbour Ltd [1942] UKHL 4: illegality
Gamerco SA v ICM/Fair Warning (Agency) Ltd [1995]: money recoverable under the act is at the discretion of the court
Herne Bay Steamboat v Hutton [1903] 2 KB 683: frustration of purpose
Howell v Coupland [1876] *1 QBD 258*: frustration if goods should come from specific source
J. Lauritzen A.S. v Wijsmuller B.V, (The Super Servant Two) [1990] 1 Lloyd's Rep: self-induced frustration
Jackson v Union Maine Insurance Co Ltd [1874] LR 10 CO 125): impossibility of adventure
Krell v Henry [1903] *2 KB 740:* frustration of purpose
Maritime National Fish Ltd v Ocean Trawlers Ltd [1935] AC 524: self-induced frustration
Metropolitan Water Board v Dick, Kerr and Co Ltd [1918] AC 119: interpretation of clause
Ocean Tramp Tankers v V/O Sovfratcht (The Eugenia) [1964] 2 QB 226: foreseeability
Paradine v Jane [1647] *Aleyn 26 KB:* contractual obligations are absolute
Robinson v Davison [1871] LR 6 Ex 269: temporary frustration
Taylor v Caldwell [1863] EWHC J1 (QB): frustration as implied term of the contract

CHAPTER XIII

BREACH OF CONTRACT AND REMEDIES

Learning Outcomes:

After reading this chapter, you should be able to understand:

- ✓ How to identify a breach of contract;
- ✓ The categorisation of contract clauses;
- ✓ The type of remedies available for breach of contract;
- ✓ How damages are calculated.

Questions and Answers:

1. How is it decided whether there is a breach of contract?

A breach of contract is a failure to perform a contractual obligation without a lawful excuse. A lawful excuse could for instance be that the contract is frustrated (See Chapter XII). Breach of contract is relatively rare as most of the time the contract is performed as agreed.

To determine whether a breach has occurred the court must examine:

- Whether there is a valid contract between the parties;
- What the rights and obligations of the parties are;
- Whether one of the parties failed to perform one of their obligations;
- Whether the contract makes any provisions for failure to perform (such as through a force majeure clause);
- Whether there was a lawful excuse not to perform this obligation;
- Whether liability for performance is limited or excluded through the contract.

Contractual liability is strict which means that the contract needs to be performed as the parties have agreed and whether the party in breach is at fault is not relevant. The motive of the person in breach is not important.

Example: Timon has a contract to deliver a package before 3pm and cannot find the location where he is supposed to go. His sat-nav is not working well so he asks people for directions who do not know either and he is driving around town trying to find the place. He finally delivers the package at 7pm. Timon clearly did his best to find the address. However, regardless of how hard he tried he has breached the contract.

This would also be the case if ***the fault is due to third parties***.

Example: Sidney has sold some flowers and needs to transport these from Colchester to Portree. He books a man with a van to take the flowers there. The van breaks down and the delivery is late, and the flowers can no longer be sold as they are spoiled. Sidney is in breach of contract with the buyer of the flowers. That a third party caused the delay does not excuse his breach of contract. At the same time the delivery company is in breach of contract with Sidney. The buyer thus has a recourse against Sidney for breach of contract, and Sidney has a recourse against the delivery company for breach of contract.

If a contract contains ***an exclusion clause for liability***, this clause will apply.

Strict liability can be contrasted with ***fault-based liability:*** The contracting party should try to fulfil his obligations with reasonable skill and care, but he is not in breach if he does not succeed.

Example: Jane goes to the hairdresser. She has a picture of a famous popstar with her. She asks the hairdresser to make her hair look the same as that. As long as the hairdresser exercises his job with reasonable skill and care he will not have breached his obligations under the contract if Jane is disappointed with the result if it does not look the same. Jane might have a different hair type and face shape than the popstar or the hairdresser might not have the same dye or other equipment that the popstar's hairdresser has.

A tender of performance means that a party has tried to perform their contractual obligation, but the other party did not accept their performance (For instance, an attempt to deliver the goods by the seller but the buyer does not accept the delivery).

2. What type of obligations are there?

- Concurrent obligations: The obligations of the parties are performed at the same time.
- Condition precedent: The performance of one of the parties depends on the other party having performed a specific obligation beforehand.
- Entire obligations: One party needs to perform their entire obligation before the other party performs theirs (***Cutter v Powell [1795]***).
- Severable obligations: Performance can be separated in different instalments (for instance in case of a contract for regular deliveries).
- Conditional: The obligation depends on whether something else happens (for instance, getting planning permission).

If an entire obligation has been ***substantially performed***, the other party might need to perform their part of the contract even if the performance is not complete.

This was the case in ***Bolton v Mahadeva [1972]*** where a contract was concluded for £500 to install a heating system. Payment was due after instalment. The system was installed but was defective with some rooms not heating properly and dangerous fumes coming from the boiler. The court held that there had been no substantial performance. Therefore, the installer was not entitled to the price minus the repair costs.

This can be contrasted with ***H Dakin & Co v Lee [1916]*** where a contract was concluded for house repairs. Some of the repairs did not comply with the contract. These deficiencies were fairly minor, and the court held that there had been substantial performance, so the repairer was entitled to the price of the contract minus the repair costs.

3. What is the *de minimis* exception?

If there is a minimal difference between what the contract stipulated and how the obligation was performed, there is no breach of contract. The difference would have to be ***so minimal that in reality there is no real difference between the contract and actual performance.***

For example, in ***Shipton, Anderson & Co v Weil Bros & Co [1912]*** a contract was concluded for the sale of 4,500 tons of wheat with a permitted deviation of 10%. The shipment contained 4,950 tons and 55 lbs. In ***Margaronis Navigation Agency Ltd v Henry W Peabody & Co Ltd [1964]*** a contract was concluded for the sale of 12,600 tons. The shortfall was 12 tons (0,1% deviate). In both of these cases it was held there was no breach of contract.

The Sale of Goods Act 1979 also allows for a de minimis exception:

> Section 15(A): 'The breach is so slight that it would be unreasonable for him to reject them.'
>
> Section 30(2A): 'If the shortfall or, as the case may be, excess is so slight that it would be unreasonable for him to do so.'

4. What are the consequences of a breach of contract?

It gives the parties access to remedies which include:

- Damages
- Right to terminate the contract (in certain circumstances)
- Specific performance (in certain circumstances)
- Injunction (in certain circumstances)
- *Quantum Meruit* (in certain circumstances)

5. When has a party the right to terminate the contract?

- The parties can always end the contract if they are in agreement on termination.
- If the contract stipulates certain conditions under which it can terminated, the contract can be terminated if these conditions are met.
- A repudiatory breach, that is to say a refusal to perform, gives the innocent party the right to termination.
- The court can decide whether the contract can be terminated following a breach of contract. Whether a contract can be terminated depends on which term of the contract was breached.

Terms are classified in three categories:

- Conditions
- Warranties
- Innominate terms

With regards to consumer contracts the Consumer Rights Act 2015 allows the consumer to end the contract if the goods do not conform (Section 22) or if delivery is late (Section 28).

6. What is a condition?

A condition is ***a term of the contract that goes to the root of the contract.*** The breach of a condition gives the innocent party the right to terminate the contract.

- Statutory law holds certain terms to be conditions. See for instance, Sections 12(5A), 13(1A), 14(6) and 15(3) of the Sale of Goods Act 1979.
- Case law has classified certain terms as conditions.
- Parties can indicate in their contract whether they hold a specific term to be a condition. This can be express or implied.

In ***The Mihalis Angelos [1970]*** a charter party stipulated that the ship would be ready to load by 1 July. It was not ready until 23 July. The charterer purported to terminate the contract because the goods they had intended to ship were no longer available. The court held that the ready to load term had long been considered a condition and therefore the contract could be terminated.

The word condition is often used in phrases such as 'terms and conditions' and is therefore used as a generic way of referring to the term of the contract. This means that not every term under such a heading would be considered a condition.

Even if the parties have stipulated that a term is a condition, this is not always decisive. **The more unreasonable the results** from considering the term a condition, the less likely that the court will hold that this was the intention of the parties (***Schuler v Wickman [1974]***).

7. What is a warranty?

A warranty is ***a subsidiary term of the contract***. The breach of a warranty entitles a party to claim damages but not to terminate the contract.

Statutory law can hold certain terms to be warranties. See for instance section 12(5A) of the Sale of Goods Act 1979.

8. What is an innominate term?

These are also called ***intermediate terms***. They are terms that could be regarded as ***either a condition or a warranty***. Classification depends on the consequences of the breach of the term.

They were first recognised in ***Hong Kong Fir v Kawaski Kishen Kaisha [1962]***. This concerned a time charter for 24 months. The contract contained a seaworthiness clause that stated that the ship was 'in every way fitted for ordinary cargo service.' However, the ship was not in a good condition and 15 weeks of the charter were lost because of repairs. The charterers terminated the contracted. The court held that the breach of the term could have different consequences, some trivial and some serious. Therefore, the court decided to look at the specific consequences for the charterers, rather than first decide whether the term was a condition or a warranty. The court held that the consequences were not sufficiently severe because considerable time still remained on the charterparty. Therefore, the charterers were only entitled to damages.

The use of innominate terms creates more uncertainty for the parties, but also ensures that the remedies for breach are proportionate to the effect of the breach. It gives the court more flexibility in deciding whether they will allow a party to escape the contract.

The court would usually decide whether a term is a condition or warranty by looking at:

- Statute
- Caselaw
- The contract itself

If none of these are conclusive, then it would be seen as an innominate term.

9. Why is it important to qualify terms?

The qualification of the term is important because if a term is classified as a condition the contract can be terminated.

If a term is a condition, it does not matter whether the actual consequences from the breach are minor. For instance, in ***Arcos v Ronaassen [1933]*** the contract was for wooden staves ½ inch thick. Some of the staves that were delivered were 1/8 inch thicker. They were perfectly suitable for the purpose for which they were bought (the construction of barrels). In ***Re Moore & Co v Landauer & Co [1921]*** peaches were supplied in cases of 24 rather than cases of 30 as specified by the contract. The amount and quality of peaches was exactly the same as was contracted for.

Both of these breaches were classified as a breach of a condition. The contract could thus be terminated, even though there were no serious consequences from the breach.

10. How do you terminate the contract?

The innocent party is not under an obligation to terminate the contract when a condition is breached. They can elect to ***terminate or affirm the contract.***

If the innocent party elects to terminate they should communicate this to the other party within a reasonable time frame (***Vitol v SA v Norelf Ltd [1996]***). ***This communication does not need to be in any particular format, but it cannot be through silence.***

Once the contract is affirmed it can then not be terminated unless the breach continues after affirmation (***Johnson v Agnew [1980]***). If the contract is affirmed and later the innocent party breaches the contract, the earlier breach of contract by the other party cannot serve as an excuse for non-performance.

Affirmation is only possible if the innocent party can still perform their obligations. Where the performance of the contract is dependent on cooperation from the breaching party affirmation is not possible (***Hounslow London Borough Council v Twickenham Garden Developments, [1971]***).

If performance is still possible, the innocent party can sue for the price of the contract. This is allowed but in exceptional circumstances, the court would need to establish whether ***the innocent party had a legitimate interest in affirmation*** (***White & Carter (Councils) Ltd v McGregor [1962]***). If affirmation is unreasonable, it is not available (***Ocean Marine Navigation Ltd v Koch Carbon Inc. - The Dynamic) [2003]***).

11. What is an anticipatory breach?

One of the parties has informed the other that they will not perform their obligations under the contract.

If a party mistakenly thought they had the right to terminate the contract this can be an anticipatory breach, but this depends on how urgent the consequences for the innocent party are (***Woodar Investments Ltd v Wimpey Construction (UK) Ltd [1980]*** and ***Federal Commerce and Navigations Co Ltd v Molena Alpha Inc [1975]***).

The innocent party may sue for breach of contract, whether or not the time for performance has come (***Hochster v De la Tour [1853]***). They may also choose to disregard the repudiation and the contract will remain in full effect.

12. What are damages?

A breach of contract by one party gives the other party the right to claim damages. If a claimant has suffered no loss, they are only entitled to recover nominal damages. ***Nominal damages*** are a symbolic sum (often £1) that recognises there was a breach of contract.

Damages are not awarded to punish the party in breach, but ***to compensate the innocent party for their loss***. Lord Scott in ***The Golden Victory [2007]*** said *"The lodestar is that the damages should represent the value of the contractual benefits of which the claimant had been deprived by the breach of contract, no less but also, no more."*

There are different ways of measuring damages:

- Expectation measures
- Reliance measures

It is also possible to pursue ***an action for the price of the contract***. That is considered a contractual debt rather than a claim for damages. This is done when one party has performed their obligations, but the other party has not paid the money they are due to pay under the contract. For a contractual debt there is no obligation to mitigate loss and the rules on remoteness of damages do not apply.

Restitution is possible if there is a total failure of consideration. A total failure of consideration does not mean that the innocent party has enjoyed no benefits under the contract, just not the ones negotiated for under the contract.

An action to enforce contractual rights need to be enforced in a specific time frame (Limitation Act 1980: 6 years for simple contracts, 12 years for a deed).

13. What are expectation measures?

Performance or expectation damages have the goal to put the innocent party in the place they would have been in if the contract had been performed as intended. They compensate the party for the loss they have suffered.

The key authority is ***Robinson v Harman [1848]***: *"The rule of the common law is, that where a party sustains loss by reason of a breach of contract, he is, so far as money can do it to be placed in the same situation, with respect to damages, as if the contract had been performed."*

Two key questions should be asked.

1. How well off would the claimant be if the contract had been performed?
2. How well off is the claimant now?

The difference is the measure of damages.

Cost of cure: The innocent party is awarded the amount it costs to cure the breach of contract

Difference in value: The innocent party is awarded the difference in value between what they received and what they could have expected under the contract.

14. What are reliance measures?

These are the expenditures made in reliance on the contract. They restore a party to the position they would be in if the contract had never happened (recovery of costs made).

Reliance measures are usually claimed when profits from the contract are uncertain and therefore it is difficult to know what position the innocent party would be in if the contract had been performed as intended.

In ***Anglia Television v Reed [1972]*** the actor Robert Reed entered into a contract with Anglia Television to play the main role in a made for television movie. The company hired different employees, scouted locations, wrote the script, and made other preparations for the movie. A few days before filming was due to start Reed announced he was no longer playing the role. He could not be replaced, and the studio abandoned the movie. He was sued for breach of contract. It would be impossible in this case to establish how much the movie would have made or even if it would have made a profit at all. The television studio therefore claimed reliance measures and sought to recover all wasted expenditure. Reed argued he should only be liable for expenditures made after he had signed the contract.

Lord Denning: *"It is true that, if the defendant had never entered into the contract, he would not be liable, and the expenditure would have been incurred by the plaintiff without redress; but the defendant having made his contract and broken it, it does not lie in his mouth to say he is not liable, when it was because of his breach that the expenditure has been wasted."*

Therefore, all expenditure could be recovered, including that incurred before the contract is concluded. The expenditure that can be recovered is that which flows from the breach and not from the formation of the contract (***Bunny v Hopkinson [1859]***).

Reliance measures are not available if ***the expected benefit from the contract is too low to cover expenditure***. They are not meant to help someone escape a bad bargain.

In ***C&P Haulage v Middleton [1983]*** a man rented a garaged with a 6-month tenancy. One of the clauses stated that he needed to return the garage to the same state as it was in when he rented it. For the tenant to be able to use the garage he needed to install some equipment and make some changes to the garage. 10 weeks before his lease was up, the owners terminated the agreement. The tenant wanted to recover his wasted expenditure which included all the changes he made to the garage. The court held that as he was obliged to return the garage to its original state at the end of the contract, he could not claim these costs as he would have spent them anyway if the contract had been performed as agreed.

The claimant should not be put in a better position than he would have been in if the contract had been performed as agreed. The defendant should prove that the expenditure was wasted (***CCC Films (London) Ltd v Impact Quadrant Ltd [1985]***).

15. What is cost of cure?

The innocent party is awarded ***damages to cure the defect in the contract***. Cost of cure is not available if disproportionate to the loss as courts are reluctant to award excessive damages.

In ***Ruxley v Forsyth [1996]*** the plaintiff was contracted to build a swimming pool which was to be 7 feet and 6 inches deep. The plaintiff made it 6 feet deep. There was no real difference in value between what the defendant received and what he contracted for. The pool could be used for swimming and diving. Claiming difference in value would have led to the defendant only receiving nominal damages. They therefore claimed cost of cure. The court held that this would be unreasonable. Cost of cure would cost more than the pool itself (because the pool needed to be broken down and then rebuild). This was disproportionate to the loss suffered. Furthermore, it was clear that the defendants would not actually use the cost of cure to rebuild the pool, but just pocket the money. Whilst this of itself is not an issue (an award for damages can be used by the recipient how they want) it showed that the defendant himself considered he had suffered no real loss. At the same time the court was also reluctant to award the difference in value because that would have meant the plaintiff would have been able to breach the contract without any real consequences.

The trial court decided to award ***a loss for amenity*** instead (£2,500 instead of the £21,560 it would cost to rebuild the pool). This was confirmed by the House of Lords. ***The intentions of the defendant*** do play a role in decision making. Oliver J in ***Radford v de Froberville [1977]:***

"First, am I satisfied on the evidence that the plaintiff has a genuine and serious intention of doing the work? Secondly, is the carrying out of the work on his own land a reasonable thing for the plaintiff to do? (…)."

16. How can a loss of chance or opportunity be measured?

Damages are recoverable for the loss of a chance or opportunity. This also applies to the chance to avoid a liability. This chance should not be merely speculative, but it should be a real substantial chance (***Maples Group Ltd v. Simmons & Simmons [1995]***). Damages are calculated based on how likely the chance and how much profit could have been made.

Chaplin v Hicks [1911] is a key authority. A young woman entered a contest of which the price was to feature in a film. 6,000 people entered and she was among the 50 people shortlisted for 12 roles. The organisers failed to inform her on time that she had been selected, so the young woman missed the final round. The court held that she was entitled to damages for loss of chance, as she had a 1 in 4 chance of winning.

17. How are damages awarded for non-pecuniary loss?

The main issue is that these are difficult to quantify and calculate. ***Non-pecuniary loss can usually not be recovered*** (***Addis v Gramophone Co Ltd [1909]*** but there are some exceptions.

Damages for harm to reputation cannot be recovered (***Addis v Gramophone [1909]***) as this would go beyond compensation and has a punitive character. The tort of defamation would be the right basis for these claims. The compensation is not for the manner of the breach but for the consequences coming from the breach. If there is ***an actual financial loss from defamation following breach of contract, then that loss can be recovered*** (***Ariel Advertising v Batchelor Peas [1938]***).

In ***Malik v BCCI [1998]*** a banker lost his job after a huge fraud was uncovered at the bank. The banker himself was completely innocent and had nothing to do with the fraud. Losing his job in this manner was very stressful, but he was also unable to find a new job because the name of his former employer was tainted. The court held that the employment contract had an implied term that the bank would do its business in all honesty. The fraudulent behaviour of the bank was thus a breach of contract. The defamation itself did not entitle him to damages, but that it seriously hurt his chances to find a new job entitled the banker to compensation.

In some cases, non-pecuniary loss can be recovered:

- Damages for pain and loss (***Godley v Perry [1960]***).
- Physical inconvenience (***Hobbs v London & South Western Railway [1875]***).
- Loss of amenity (***Ruxley v Forsyth [1996]***).
- *Loss of enjoyment* where the very object of the contract is enjoyment or relaxation (***Jarvis v Swan Tours [1973]***).

Bingham LJ in ***Watts v Morrow [1991]***:

1) *If the very object of the contract is to provide pleasure, relaxation, peace of mind, or freedom for molestation but due to the defendant's breach the contrary result is procured instead.*
2) *For physical inconvenience and discomfort caused by the breach and mental suffering directly related to that inconvenience and discomfort.*

This was broadened in ***Farley v Skinner [2001]*** and ***pleasure/relaxation now only needs to be one of the objectives of the contract.*** The plaintiff employed the defendant to survey a property that he wanted to purchase as a secondary residence. The property was located 15 miles from Gatwick Airport and the plaintiff asked the surveyor to report on any disturbance by aircraft noise. The surveyor advised that the house was unlikely to be affected by the noise. The plaintiff bought the house and spent £100,000 to improve it. He then discovered that there was a lot of noise from the airport. He brought an action for breach of contract.

The House of Lords held that the plaintiff was entitled to damages because relaxation, peace of mind, and pleasure were an important part of the contract and there was no need for these to be the 'very object of the contract.' The plaintiff had clearly indicated how important this was to him which made the report on noise a contractual obligation for the surveyor.

Courts are restrictive in how high the awards should be in these cases because they should not be so high as to have a punitive character.

Loss of enjoyment and mental distress can only be claimed for consumer contracts (***Hayes v James & Charles Rodd [1990]***). This reflects that consumers often contract for other reasons than purely financial.

18. How are damages calculated?

There must be a causal link between the wrongdoing and the loss. ***The breach must be the actual cause of the loss.*** But for the breach, the loss would not have occurred. This is useful to establish whether there is a connection between the breach and the loss.

There is a difference between a breach of contract causing a loss and one causing ***an opportunity for loss to occur***. In ***Quinn v Burch Bros (Builders) Ltd. [1966]*** the defendant failed to supply a stepladder and the plaintiff used a folded trestle as a makeshift ladder. He injured himself. The court held that the loss was the plaintiff's own doing although the defendant created the opportunity for the loss.

Novus actus interveniens: An intervening act made possible by the breach. This can break the link of causation. In ***Lambert v Lewis [1982]*** a farmer bought a towing hitch. He discovered it was defective, but he continued to use it. One day it broke and caused an accident killing one person and injuring another. The farmer wanted to hold the seller responsible for the accident. However, because the farmer had kept using the hitch even after he found out it was defective the link of causation was broken. The seller was not responsible for the accident because of the interfering act.

If the party in breach is found to be negligent thus allowing for the loss to occur, he could still be responsible regardless of the intervening act.

If there is a concurrent liability in tort and in contract, the reduction for ***contributory negligence*** as per the Contributory Negligence Act 1945 also applies for liability in contract. That does not apply to strict liability obligations, and it also does not apply to fault-based liability if there is no independent liability in tort (***Forsikringsaktieselskapet Vesta v Butcher [1986]***). It therefore has limited usage.

Loss is compensated if it flows naturally from the breach, if it is not too remote, and if it was foreseeable. Remoteness is based on the knowledge of the parties at the moment of contracting.

Hadley v Baxendale [1854] established the key principle for ***remoteness of damages.*** A crankshaft was delivered to a mill in Greenwich, 5 days later than the contract stipulated. The owners of the mill sued the carriers for loss of 5 days' profit. The court held that the loss was too remote because the carriers only knew that the equipment needed to be delivered but they did not know that the mill would not be operational if the delivery was delayed.

Only ordinary loss can be recovered. In ***Victoria Laundry (Windsor) v Newman Industries [1949]*** a laundry bought a new boiler to expand their business. The laundry had a lucrative new contract with the government. The seller delivered the boiler 5 months late. The buyer sued for loss of profit which included £16 a week for normal profits and £262 a week for loss of the government contract. The seller was held liable for the £16 loss as they knew the boiler was needed to keep the business operational. They were not held liable for the £262 loss because they could not have known about the government contract.

Only ordinary and foreseeable loss from the breach can be claimed. However, if the buyers had told the sellers about the government contract when concluding the new boiler contract, the sellers could have been held responsible as they would have been able to foresee the loss.

The remoteness test is an objective one and the foreseeability should be 'highly likely' and 'a serious possibility' (***Koufos v C. Czarnikow Ltd (he Heron II) [1969]***). The test for foreseeability is higher in contract than in tort, because in contract the parties can communicate possible losses when entering into the contract.

It is ***the type of losses*** that should have been contemplated by the parties and not the extent of the loss (***Parsons (Livestock) Ltd v Uttley Ingham &Co Ltd [1978]***).

Physical damage and financial damage should be treated the same way, but physical damage often also gives rise to a claim of negligence in tort. If there are concurrent liabilities in tort and negligence, the foreseeability test should be the same for both (***Wellesley Partners LLP v Withers LLP [2015]***).

A different approach to remoteness emerged in ***Transfield Shipping Inc v Mercator Shipping Inc (The Achilleas) [2008]***. On a time charter the ship was returned 9 days late. The owners of the ship already concluded a follow-on charter for a period of 191 days. Because the ship was late, the follow-on charter could not start on time and had to be renegotiated. Because of fluctuations in the market the price for the new charter was reduced by $8,000 a day. The ship owners then sued the first charterers for the price difference: $8,000 x 191 days = $1,364,584. The defendant charterers argued that they should only be liable for the price difference for the 9 days they were late and not the 191 days: $158,301.17.

The House of Lords held that the defendants would only be liable for the 9 days, because the losses were too remote: ***The defendant had not assumed responsibility for the loss.*** It had not been the intention of the parties which could be interfered from the market context. In the shipping industry the custom is that the party in breach is liable for the contractual price or the market price (whichever is higher) for the actual days of the delay.

Hadley v Baxendale is still good law. It is a prima facie rule that can be rebutted. It remains the general rule, while ***the assumption of liability rule laid down in the Achilleas is confined to unusual cases*** (***Sylvia Shipping Co Ltd v Progress Bulk Carriers Ltd (the Sylvia) [2010]***).

19. How is loss mitigated?

In case of a breach of the contract, ***the innocent party should take reasonable steps to mitigate their losses or to not unreasonably increase their losses.*** If loss is not mitigated the innocent party cannot recover damages for losses that could have been prevented by taking reasonable steps.

Example: Laura contracts with Fei to buy 5,000 Christmas trees. The agreed delivery date is 2 December. The trees do not arrive until December 28. Laura will not be able to sell the trees for the same price now that they are not in demand as Christmas is over. Laura manages to sell the trees for 15% of the original value. Fei is responsible for paying the remaining 85%. If Laura had not taken reasonable steps to sell the trees, she still would only have been able to recuperate 85% as she has an obligation to mitigate her losses.

In ***Brace v Calder [1895]*** the plaintiff was employed for a period of 2 years as a manager of a partnership. Two months into his contract two members of the partnership retired and the partnership was dissolved. The plaintiff was dismissed. The remaining two partners started a new business and they offered to re-employ the plaintiff. The plaintiff rejected the offer and sued. The court held that the plaintiff had failed to mitigate his losses when he refused the offer and was therefore entitled to only nominal damages.

When mitigating his losses, the innocent party should take into account other stakeholders such as shareholders (***Banco de Portugal v Waterlow and Sons ltd [1932]***) and does not have to engage in risky activities (***Pikington v Wood [1953]***) or violate morality or attract negative attention (***James Finley and Co v NV Kwik Hoo Tong Handelsmaatschappij [1929]***).

20. What is the date of assessment for damages?

Damages are assessed at ***the date of the breach of contract***. That is the day that the innocent party could have to source substitute performance. The difference between the price of the contract and the market price on the day of breach is the measurement for damages.

This is not an absolute rule and sometimes the date is postponed for instance because the innocent party did not have the resources to purchase a substitute performance and the prices in that particular market fluctuate substantially. Lord Wilberforce in ***Johnson v Agnew [1980]***: *"if to follow [the rule] would give rise to injustice, the court has power to fix such other date as may be appropriate in the circumstances."*

21. What is meant with account for profits?

A party to the contract might profit from a breach of contract. The claimant can generally not recover this.

Example: Ulysses is selling his motorcycle. He concludes a contract with Darya for £1,500. Ciaran offers Ulysses £2,000 for the motorcycle. Ulysses decides to breach the contract with Darya. Darya can now sue Ulysses for breach of contract. Darya can claim back whatever loss she has suffered: The same type of motorcycle can be bought for £1,750. Buying this motorcycle would put Darya in the position she would have had if the contract had been performed as planned. If she has made no additional costs, the measure of damages would likely be £1,750. Ulysses is therefore £250 better off because Ciaran gave him £2,000. His contract with Ciaran is separate and he does not owe Darya the £250 profits.

This can lead to parties breaching a contract on purpose because the benefit from breaching the contract outweighs the losses from the breach (***efficiency breach***).

In exceptional cases the court can require ***an account for profits***. This is often for reasons of public policy. The leading case is ***Attorney General v Blake [2001]***. A secret service agent defected and became a spy for the Soviet Union When he was in the secret service, he signed a non-disclosure agreement. He breached this agreement by writing a book about his experiences. The court held that Blake should not profit from the breach of contract and the sum the publisher paid to Blake in advance of the book being published was recoverable.

It is only available if damages are inadequate. In the above example the state had suffered no loss from Blake's breach of contract. Therefore, damages would only be nominal and not an adequate remedy.

A key question the court will ask is whether ***the innocent party has a legitimate interest in depriving the party in breach from their profit.***

It is used very seldom and almost never in commercial law cases. One exception is ***Esso Petroleum Co Ltd v Niad Ltd [2001]*** where the owner of an Esso Petroleum station entered into a contract with Esso regarding a price guarantee scheme. If the price for petroleum was lower at competing gas stations, the petrol station would also lower its price in return for cheaper petroleum from Esso. The petrol station did not reduce its prices on several occasions. Esso could not show how much it had lost from a single station not reducing its prices. The court held that an account for profits was justifiable because other remedies were inadequate, and it could undermine the entire scheme which was popular with customers. Therefore, Esso had a legitimate interest in claiming the profits.

This decision was criticised because the legitimate interest ground was applied far wider than in ***Blake v AG***. ***Esso*** has not been followed widely and subsequent caselaw has restricted account for profit further (***Morris-Garner v One-Step Support Ltd [2018]***).

22. Is it possible for the parties to agree in advance about which damages should be paid?

The parties can include a ***liquidated damages*** clause in their contract. In that clause they can stipulate a sum of money to be paid in the event of a breach. It can be distinguished from a ***penalty clause*** which contains a sum that is exorbitant and highly disproportional to the breach. Penalty clauses are not enforceable in English contract law.

The following aspects are taken into account in deciding whether the clause should be allowed:

- Is it a secondary obligation (that is to say an obligation that arises when a primary obligation is breached)?
- Is there a genuine pre-estimate of the loss (***Dunlop Pneumatic Tyre Co Ltd v New Garage and Motor Co Ltd [1915]***)?

- If it is not a genuine pre-estimate: Does it protect a legitimate interest of the party that inserted the clause (***Cavendish Square Holding BV v Talal El Madessi [2015]***)?
- Is it proportional, given the context of the contract?

23. What is specific performance?

The court makes an order ***compelling a contractual party to do what they contracted to do.*** It is only granted when damages are inadequate to compensate for the party's loss. In English contract law it is a ***secondary equitable remedy*** whereas in civil law countries it is often a primary remedy; including in Scotland where it is called specific implement. In English contract law specific performance is granted at the discretion of the court; therefore, it is not granted of rights like damages.

It is often ordered for the sale of unique objects such as art and the sale of land. It can also be ordered if the object is not unique but there is no other availability on the market (***Sky Petroleum Ltd v VIP Petroleum Ltd [1974]***).

It can also be ordered if an obligation to pay is not enforceable such as in ***Beswick v Beswick [1968]*** where a man sold his business to his nephew. If the uncle died, the nephew had to pay weekly instalments of £5 to his aunt. The uncle died and the nephew did not pay. The aunt could not enforce the contract as she was not a contracting party. The uncle's estate was a party and could enforce the contract. However, the estate had suffered no loss and could only get nominal damages. This would not help the aunt. The court therefore ordered specific performance of the contract, and this allowed the aunt to get the weekly payments.

Courts will not mandate specific performance for personal service contracts (such as employment). See Trade Union and Labour Relations (Consolidation) Act 1992, Section 236.

Specific performance will not be granted if it causes ***undue hardship.*** In ***Patel v Ali [1984]*** the defendant entered into a contract to sell her house to the plaintiff. The sale did not happen because the defendant's husband became bankrupt, and an injunction was obtained against the completion of the sale. Three years later the sale could be completed. By then her husband was in jail and the defendant herself had become disabled and needed support. The court held that it would cause her undue hardship if she had to sell her house as she needed her home and the support of her neighbours and friends.

Courts usually do not order specific performance if it would require ***constant supervision*** by the court. In ***Co-operative Insurance Society Ltd v Argyll***

Stores [1990] the defendant owned a supermarket located in a mall owned by the plaintiff. The contract stipulated that the defendant should keep the supermarket open for retail trade. The supermarket ran at a loss and the defendant decided to close it. The plaintiff sued for specific performance. If granted the defendant would have to keep operating the supermarket even if this was at a loss. The court held that it would cause significant losses to the defendant. Furthermore, the order would require constant court supervision and could lead to a myriad of claims.

The Sale of Goods Act 1979, Section 52 gives the court discretion to order specific performance in relation to non-delivery of goods.

For ***consumer contracts*** there are specific rules on specific performance (See Consumer Rights Act 2015). Consumers are entitled to repair or replacement. They can choose either unless one is impossible or disproportionate.

If:

1. Repair or replacement are not possible;
2. Repair or replacement was attempted but failed;
3. Repair or replacement was not provided within reasonable time.

The consumer can opt for a price reduction or can reject the goods.

24. What is an injunction?

This is another equitable and discretionary remedy

There are two kinds:

Prohibitory injunction – an order prohibiting a party from acting in a certain way (for instance, to breach the contract)

Mandatory Injunction – an order mandating a party to do something (available under the same conditions as specific performance)

25. What are negotiated damages or hypothetical bargain damages?

These are damages that ***compensate for the loss of a valuable asset or fee*** (***Morris-Garner v One-Step Support Ltd [2018]***). They represent the amount that could have been negotiated. They are available in lieu of an injunction.

The key authority is ***Wrotham Park Estate Co v Parkside Homes Ltd [1974]*** where a developer bought a piece of land which was subject to several restrictions. The houses were built in a way that breached the restrictions. The seller sued the developer. The question was how to compensate the seller. It was difficult to assess the damages because the seller has suffered no real loss.

The developer was expecting to make extra profit because of the breach. The court awarded the seller 5% of that extra profit on the basis that this was the amount they would likely have obtained if they had negotiated with the developer on excluding the restrictions from the contract.

26. What is *quantum meruit?*

This means 'as much deserved.' It is used to provide ***remuneration to a party for performance*** under a contract such as where goods have been delivered or a service was provided, but no payment was received, and this payment cannot be obtained under the contract. Traditionally the term *quatum meruit* is used for services and the similar action *quantum valebat* is used for goods, but the effects are the same.

Quantum meruit aims to pay for performance but not to compensate for loss as is the case for damages. The court will order that a reasonable sum (usually the market price) should be paid for the performance.

Quantum meruit is often used in situations where:

- Additional work was requested by the defendant outside of the contract.
- There is a quasi-contract.
- The work was performed under a void, unenforceable or terminated contract.
- There is an accepted repudiatory breach.

Summary:

- If a condition is breached the contract can be terminated, and if a warranty is breached only damages can be claimed. For innominate terms it depends on the consequences of the breach.
- Performance measures seek to compensate the innocent party for their loss and put them in the place they would be in if the contract had been performed as agreed.
- Reliance measures aim to recover all the wasted expenditure and put the innocent party in the position they would have had, if the contract had never been concluded.
- Damages can only be claimed for loss that is not too remote, was foreseeable, and flows naturally from the breach. In exceptional cases the court will also look at whether the parties had assumed responsibility for the loss.
- Non-pecuniary loss can only be compensated in very specific circumstances.

- Whilst damages are available by right other remedies such as specific performance, injunction, and account for profits are equitable measures which are only available at the discretion of the court if damages would not compensate adequately.
- Liquidated damages clauses are allowed but should not have a punitive character.

Key Cases

Addis v Gramophone Co Ltd [1909] AC 488: non-pecuniary loss
Anglia Television v Reed [1972] *1QB*: example of reliance measures
Arcos v EA Ronaasen & Son [1933] AC 470: breach of a condition
Attorney General v Blake [2001] 1AC 268: account for profits
Beswick v Beswick [1968] *AC 58:* specific performance in third party cases
Bolton v Mahadeva [1972] *1 WLR 1009:* no entitlement to pay if performance not substantive
Brace v Calder [1895] *2 QB 253:* mitigation of losses
C&P Haulage v Middleton [1983] *1 WLR 1461*: reliance measures not available if expenditure does not outweigh potential benefit
Cavendish Square Holding BV v Talal El Madessi [2015] *UKSC 6*: legitimate interest in liquidated damages clause
CCC Films (London) Ltd v Impact Quadrant Films Ltd [1985] QB 16: choice between measures
Chaplin v Hicks [1911] *2 KB 786*: loss of opportunity
Co-operative Insurance Society Ltd v Argyll Stores [1990] *AC 1:* constant supervision by the court of specific performance
Dunlop Pneumatic Tyre Co Ltd v New Garage and Motor Co Ltd [1915] AC 79: genuine pre-estimate of loss
Esso Petroleum Co Ltd v Niad Ltd [2001] All ER (D) 324: accounts for profit
Farley v Skinner [2001] *UK HL 49*: pleasure/enjoyment should be a substantial object
Forsikringsaktieselskapet Vesta v Butcher [1986] *2 All ER 488*: contributory negligence only if independent liability in tort
Godley v Perry [1960] *1 WLR 1461:* damages for pain and loss
Golden Strait Corporation v Nippon Yusen Kubishika Kaisha (The Golden Victory) [2007] UKHL 12: affirmation of compensatory principle of damages
H Dakin & Co v Lee [1916] *1 KB 566:* entitlement to pay if performance substantive
Hadley v Baxendale [1854] 9 Exch 341: foreseeability of loss
Hayes v James & Charles Rodd [1990] *2 All ER 815*: mental distress can only be claimed for consumer contracts
Hobbs v London & Southwestern Railway [1875] LR 10 QB: damages for physical inconvenience
Hochster v De la Tour [1853] 22 LJQB 4 SS: anticipatory breach
Hong Kong Fir v Kawaski Kishen Kaisha [1962] 2QB 26: innominate terms
Hounslow LBC v Twickenham Garden Developments Ltd [1971] *Ch 23*: affirmation only possible if not dependent upon both parties performing
Jarvis v Swan Tours [1973] QB 233: compensation for loss of enjoyment
Johnson v Agnew [1980] *AC 367:* date of assessment of damages
Koufos v C. Czarnikow Ltd (he Heron II) [1969] 1 AC 350: foreseeability should be highly likely
L Schuler AG v Wickman Machine Tools Sales Ltd [1974] *AC 235*: intention of the parties in deciding whether a term is a condition
Lambert v Lewis [1982] *AC 225:* interfering act breaches link of causality
Malik v Bank of Credit and Commerce International [1998] *AC 20:* actual financial loss coming from defamation can be recovered
Maples Group Ltd v. Simmons & Simmons [1995] *4 All ER 907*: chance should be real and not merely speculative

Maredelanto Compania Naviera SA v Bergbau-Handel GmbH (The Mihalis Angelos) [1970] EWCA Civ 4: termination of contract because breach of a condition

Margaronis Navigation Agency Ltd v Henry W Peabody & Co Ltd [1964] 1 Lloyd's Rep 173: de minimis exception

Morris-Garner v One-Step Support Ltd [2018] UKSC 20: limitation of accounts for profit

Morris-Garner v One-Step Support Ltd [2018] UKSC 20: negotiated damages

Ocean Marine Navigation Ltd v Koch Carbon Inc. (The Dynamic) [2003] EWHC 1936: affirmation should only not be allowed when unreasonable

Parsons (Livestock) Ltd v Uttley Ingham &Co Ltd [1978] 1QB 79: Type of loss

Patel v Ali [1984] *1 All ER 978*: specific performance causing undue hardship

Quinn v Burch Bros. (Builders) Ltd [1966] 2 QB 370: opportunity for loss

Radford v De Froberville [1977] *1 WLR 1262*: cost of cure/intentions of the innocent party

Re Moore & Landauer [1921] 2 KB 519: breach of a condition

Robinson v Harman [1848] *1 Ex Rep 850*: purpose of damages is compensatory

Ruxley v Forsyth [1996] *1 AC 344*: loss of amenity/cost of cure

Shipton, Anderson & Co v Weil Bros & Co [1912] 1 KB 574: de minimis exception

Sky Petroleum Ltd v VIP Petroleum Ltd [1974] 1 WLR 576: specific performance in case of non-availability of goods

Sumpter v Hedges [1898] *1QB 673*: entire obligations

Sylvia Shipping Co Ltd v Progress Bulk Carriers Ltd (the Sylvia) [2010] EWHC s42 (Comm): assumption of liability confined to unusual cases

Transfield Shipping Inc v Mercator Shipping Inc (The Achilleas) [2008] UKHL 48: assumption of liability

Victoria Laundry (Windsor) Ltd v Newman Industries Ltd [1949] 2 KB 528: only ordinarily foreseeable loss can be compensated

Vitol SA v Norelf Ltd, The Santa Clare [1996] AC 800: termination must be communicated

Watts v Morrow [1991] *WLR 1421*: non-pecuniary loss

Wellesley Partners LLP v Withers LLP [2015] *EWCA Civ 114:* concurrent liabilities in tort and contract

White & Carter (Councils) Ltd v McGregor [1962] AC 413: legitimate interest in affirmation

Wrotham Park Estate Co v Parkside Homes Ltd [1974] WLR 798: negotiated damages

SUMMARY: SAMPLE MULTIPLE CHOICE QUESTIONS

FORMATION OF THE CONTRACT

1. Goods on display in a shop are considered to be an:

a) Offer
b) Acceptance
c) Invitation to treat
d) Request for information

2. If an offer is accepted by postal letter, when does acceptance take effect?

a) On receipt
b) On dispatch in all cases
c) On dispatch, but only if the acceptance by post would have been contemplated by the parties
d) When the offeror reads the letter

3. Bella tells Lisette she is selling her bike for £300. Lisette says that she will buy the bike for £250. What is Lisette's statement?

a) An acceptance
b) An invitation to treat
c) A counteroffer
d) A request for information

4. Sebastian has lost his engagement ring. He puts an advertisement in the local paper offering anyone who will find the ring a reward of £100. Christian finds the ring and brings it back to Sebastian. Sebastian tells Christian that as he and his partner had a huge fight, they are not getting married and he no longer needs the ring. He does not want to give the reward money to Christian. Which statement is correct?

a) Christian never told Sebastian he accepted the offer, so he is not entitled to the reward.
b) Christian accepted Sebastian's offer through returning the ring and therefore he is entitled to the reward.
c) A newspaper advertisement is never an offer, it was just an invitation to treat.

d) Sebastian no longer needs the ring and therefore he can revoke his offer.

5. Helena knows that Penny loves Helena's car, a Jeep Cherokee. Penny has often said to Helena that she would love to have the same car and that she would be interested in buying the car if Helena ever wanted to sell. Helena has just gotten a new car and she decides to sell the Jeep to Penny. She sends Penny a text: 'Jeep Cherokee is yours for £20,000. If I do not hear from you by Sunday to say otherwise it is yours.' Which statement is incorrect?

a) If Penny does not get in touch with Helena, she is legally bound to buy Helena's car.
b) If Penny gets in touch with Helena to say that she accepts, Helena is bound by her offer.
c) If Penny does not get in touch with Helena, she is not legally bound to buy the car.
d) If Helena changes her mind she needs to get in touch with Penny and revoke the offer

6. Which case is authority for the fact that consideration must be sufficient but need not be adequate?

a) Stilk v Myrick [1809]
b) Chappell Co Ltd v Nestle Co Ltd [1960]
c) Lampleigh v Braithwaite [1615]
d) Tweedle v Atkinson [1861]

7. Fleur asks her employee Milan to do some overtime to finish a report. Milan works 10 additional hours and finishes the report. Fleur is very happy and promises Milan, she will give him a £150 in recognition of his work. Fleur later refuses to pay. Which statement is most likely correct regarding Milan's position?

a) Fleur does not have to pay Milan because the promise was made after he had done the work and therefore the consideration is past.
b) Fleur does not have to pay Milan because Milan was just doing her a favour.
c) Fleur should pay Milan because she asked him to do the overtime and it would have been reasonable to expect that this was paid.
d) Fleur should pay Milan because it does not matter when the consideration is given, as long as there is consideration.

8. Georgie is opening his new campground with a big celebration. The campground is in a natural preservation area. Environmental activists are against the campground because they fear that all the people coming there will destroy the flowers and frighten the wildlife. Georgie is afraid the environmental activists will protest at the opening and disturb the festivities. Georgie asks the police for support. The police judges that the activists are not a real threat, and they therefore will not send any police on the day. Georgie asks the police if they will send two officers if he pays £2,000. The police agree. The festivities pass without any problems and only a few environmentalists come to protest peacefully and do not offer a threat. The police officers do not have to do anything, and they can enjoy being part of the celebration, they eat and dance along with everyone else. Georgie refuses to pay. Which statement is correct?

a) The police cannot claim the money promised by Georgie as they have a public duty to maintain law and order.
b) The police can claim payment because they went beyond their public duty, as they made a judgment call that extra protection would not be necessary.
c) The police cannot claim payment because the officers did not do any work.
d) The police can claim payment because even though they have a public duty to maintain law and order Georgie made a promise and that should always be honoured.

9. Which of the following statements is correct with regard to promissory estoppel in contracts?

Promissory estoppel can only be used as a sword and not a shield.

a) Promissory estoppel can only be used as a shield and not a sword.
b) Promissory estoppel can be used both as a shield and as a sword.
c) Promissory estoppel can be used as neither a shield nor a sword.

10. Teri borrowed £6,000 from Sol. Teri does not have the money to pay Sol back so she offers him £3,000 and she also offers to give him one of her home baked cakes which she knows Sol loves. Sol agrees but he later regrets the decision and wants the outstanding £3,000. Which of the following statements most accurately summarise Sol's legal position?

a) Sol is not entitled to the balance, because he agreed with Teri that the £3,000 was sufficient.

b) Sol is not entitled to the balance, because whilst part payment of debt in satisfaction of the whole is not sufficient consideration, adding the cake makes the consideration sufficient.
c) Sol is entitled to the balance, because part payment of debt in satisfaction of the whole is not sufficient consideration and the value of the cake is not sufficient to change this.
d) Sol is entitled to the balance because he did not receive any consideration in return for his agreement.

11. Andrew has contracted Kirsty to build a garden house in return for £20,000. Halfway through the work Kirsty tells Andrew that she has severe financial issues, and she will not be able to finish building it if she does not get an extra £3,000. Andrew is concerned as he needs the garden house finished as quickly as possible as he will be using it as an office for his consultancy business. He needs a place where he can work quietly and receive his customers. Andrew therefore agrees to pay Kirsty the extra money. When the garden house is finished Andrew pays the £20,000 but refuses to pay the extra £3,000. Which one of the following statements is the most likely to be true?

a) Kirsty was only performing a contractual duty she had already agreed to do and did not give any consideration for the £3,000.
b) Kirsty exceeded her contractual duty and is entitled to the extra £3,000.
c) Kirsty is entitled to the extra £3,000 because Andrew said he would pay it and he is not allowed to change his mind.
d) Kirsty is probably entitled to the extra £3,000 because Andrew derived a practical benefit from agreeing to pay the money.

12. Which of the following statements about certainty of agreement is NOT true?

a) If deleting a vague sentence does not impact on whether the contract can be performed as agreed, then it can be deleted.
b) If the court has to write the contract for the parties, the contract cannot be enforced.
c) If the parties have included a machinery to decide certain aspects, the contract cannot be enforced.
d) If the parties have not included the price the contract cannot be enforced.

13. Jonathan and Matteo are good friends. Jonathan has agreed to help Matteo take care of his horse every Monday when Matteo works. In return he can ride Matteo's horse whenever he wants. After a few months Jonathan gets too busy, and he can no longer help Matteo. Which statement most likely reflects Jonathan's legal position?

a) Jonathan should continue to help Matteo because Matteo has provided consideration.
b) Jonathan can stop helping Matteo provided he gives him at least a month notice.
c) This is a social arrangement, and it is unlikely the court will find that they intended to create legal relations.
d) This is a social arrangement, but because Jonathan has already helped Matteo for several months and Matteo provided consideration, the presumption they did not intend to create legal relations is rebutted.

14. Which statement regarding the intention to create legal relations between partners is NOT true?

a) If the couple are no longer living in amity when they made the arrangement it is likely binding.
b) Provided that the contract meets all the criteria for an enforceable contract it is always binding.
c) If the agreement is about finances or property, it is more likely to be considered binding.
d) If the couple are living in amity, it is not likely to be binding even if subsequently, they divorce.

PRIVITY, CAPACITY, AND CONTRACTUAL TERMS

1. Which of the following statements on Section 1 of the Contracts (Rights of Third Parties) Act 1999 is true?

a) A third-party beneficiary can only sue upon the contract if they already exist at the time the contract is concluded.
b) The parties can include a clause in the contract providing the third-party beneficiary cannot sue upon the contract.
c) The third-party beneficiary can only sue upon the contract if they consented to the benefit at the time of contracting.
d) The third-party beneficiary can only sue upon the contract if his/her name is included the contract.

2. Daniel, a shopkeeper, buys a new fridge for the kitchen in his house. The seller gives him a notice stating that the buyer can return the goods within 14 days of purchase and receive a full refund and that in those cases a £50 administration charge is payable by the buyer. Daniel has not read the notice and decides that the fridge does not look nice in his kitchen and wants to return this. Which one of the following statements reflects Daniel position the best?

a) The buyer did not read the notice and is not bound by it.
b) The seller is entitled to impose the administration charge.
c) Under the Unfair Contract Terms Act 1977 s. 6, the seller has no right to impose the administration charge.
d) Under Part 2 of the Consumer Rights Act 2015, the charge could be considered an unfair contract term and will not be imposed.

3. The terms in a notice can be incorporated in the contract as long as the notice is given before or at the time of contracting

a) True.
b) False.

4. Thoby is taking the bus to Carlisle. His ticket has the following clause in clear large letters: 'the company accepts no liability in negligence for injury caused for passengers on this service.' Which one of the following statements is the most accurate?

a) The term is subject to a fairness test under the Consumer Rights Act 2015.
b) The term is binding because it is very clearly worded.
c) The term is not binding as it is not incorporated in the contract because Thoby would not have seen the term until he bought the ticket.
d) The term is not binding because it is unenforceable under the Consumer Rights Act 2015.

5. The court applies the test under Section 11 of the Unfair Contract Terms Act 1977 to determine whether an exemption clause in a B2B contract is reasonable. This test looks at the content of the term and whether other businesses use the same term.

a) True
b) False

6. Terms cannot be implied through

a) Custom
b) Statute
c) Necessity
d) Fairness

7. Can minors enter into a contract?

a) Yes, as long as the contract is fair and beneficial for the minor.
b) No, minors can never enter into a contract.
c) No, but there are certain exceptions notably contracts for necessaries and beneficiary service contracts.
d) Yes, but only with the consent of their parents/guardians.

8. Do companies have the capacity to enter into contract?

a) Yes, companies can enter into a contract in the same way as natural persons can.
b) Yes, companies can enter into a contract but only if it is in accordance with the purpose of the company.
c) No, only natural persons can enter into a contract.
d) No, unless they have permission from company's shareholders.

VITIATING FACTORS AND FRUSTRATION

1. Which of the following statements on actual undue influence is true?

a) The party seeking to rely upon actual undue influence must show that there is a relationship of trust and confidence themselves and the other party
b) There should be something unusual about the transaction
c) The party claiming actual undue influence should show that they had no choice but to agree
d) The party claiming actual undue influence should prove that the intentions of the other party are unsound

2. Which one of the following relationships is not a relationship that falls under Class 2A of undue influence

a) A parent and a child
b) A pastor and a parishioner
c) A solicitor and a client
d) A bank and a client

3. Liam threatens to kidnap Morwenna's brother if she does not agree to sell him her business. The resulting contract is:

a) Void for duress
b) Voidable for duress
c) Valid as long as Liam pays a fair price
d) Valid, but she can claim damages for distress

4. Which case introduced the notion of 'economic duress'?

a) Barton v Armstrong
b) The Sibeon & The Sibotre
c) Skeate v Beale
d) Pao In v Lau Yiu Long

5. A contract cannot be discharged by frustration if

a) An intervening event makes performance of a contract impossible.
b) An intervening event makes performance of a contract more onerous.
c) An intervening event makes performance of a contract illegal.
d) An intervening fundamentally changes the purpose of the contract.

6. Bronwyn contracts with Sufyan to rent his pub for the evening of 5 May so she can throw a birthday party for her sister. Bronwyn pays a deposit of £300 and the remaining £1,100 is due two days before the party. On May 2 the pub is destroyed in a fire. If contract is frustrated what is Bronwyn's financial position?

a) Bronwyn cannot recover the deposit and she must pay the balance of £1,100.
b) Bronwyn cannot recover the deposit, but she also does not need to pay the £1,100.
c) Bronwyn can recover half the deposit and she has to pay half the balance so that the loss is evenly distributed.
d) Bronwyn can recover the deposit and she does not have to pay the balance of £1,100.

7. Which case is the key authority on mistake as to quality?

a) Great Peace Shipping Ltd v Tsavliris Salvage (International) Ltd
b) Bell v Lever Brothers Ltd
c) Cooper v Phibbs
d) Couturier v Hastie

8. Lucy is looking at buy to let properties. The seller of a flat tells her that there are long term tenants in there who are absolutely great. Lucy decides to buy the flat and she finds out that the tenants have not paid the rent for the last five months. The seller knew this. Which statement is most accurate?

a) That the tenants are great is an opinion and will not amount to misrepresentation.
b) That the tenants are great is a statement of mere puff and will not amount to misrepresentation.
c) That the tenants are great is an opinion, but as it is factually not true it will amount to misrepresentation.
d) That the tenants are great is an opinion, and Lucy should have asked for more details about the tenants.

9. Samir buys a truck from Alexei. Alexei and Samir do not know that the truck had an accident the day before the contract was concluded. It was declared total loss. Which statement reflects most accurately the legal position of the parties?

a) The contract is void for common mistake.
b) The contract is voidable for common mistake.
c) The contract is void for unilateral mistake.
d) The contract is voidable for unilateral mistake.

10. Which of the following statements is most likely to be a statement of fact?

a) A statement by the seller of a house about whether the house has double glazing.
b) A statement made about how a certain washing powder gets even the worse stains out.
c) A statement made by one friend to the other about the need for planning permission for a loft conversion.
d) A statement made by the seller of a house about his intentions to paint the living room yellow before moving out.

BREACH OF CONTRACT AND REMEDIES

1. Which of the following is not a bar to recission?

a) Time lapse
b) Affirmation of the contract
c) No protestation at the time of contracting
d) Third party has acquired rights in good faith

2. Which case established the test of remoteness?

a) Ruxley Electronics v Forsyth
b) Victoria Laundry Ltd v Newman Industries Ltd
c) Hadley v Baxendale
d) Foakes v Beer

3. Yvette runs a restaurant. She has bought a new oven. Her old oven will be removed on the 22 September. She has contracted with Kitchen Builders to install her new over on 23 September in the morning. That way she will only lose one evening's income. Kitchen Builders are delayed, and the oven is not installed until 27 September. Yvette wants to recover the loss from the days she had to close the restaurant. She also had a wedding party booked on 25 September and needed to cancel this contract. She also wants to recover damages for this. Which statement likely reflects Yvette's position best?

a) Yvette can sue for all damages as they were all a direct result of the oven being installed later than agreed.
b) Yvette can recover the loss she has suffered from having to close the restaurant, but likely not the loss caused by the cancellation of the wedding party.
c) Yvette cannot recover any losses because it was her responsibility to get a replacement oven.
d) Yvette cannot recover any losses because the contract is frustrated.

4. Which of the following statements is correct?

a) Specific performance is a common law remedy which is available as of right, where there has been a breach of contract.
b) Specific performance is an equitable remedy and is usually only available where damages cannot adequately remedy the loss.
c) Specific performance is a primary remedy for breach of contract.
d) Specific performance is especially used for employment contracts.

5. Which of the following statements is incorrect in relation to damages at contract law?

a) Damages can be claimed for loss profit.
b) Damages are not intended to be punitive.
c) Damages can be awarded for all non-pecuniary loss.
d) Damages can be claimed for loss of chance.

6. What are the usual consequences of a breach of warranty?

a) The innocent party can claim damages.
b) The innocent party can terminate the contract.
c) The innocent party can terminate the contract and claim damages.
d) The innocent party can rescind the contract.

7. How are clauses divided?

a) Terms and conditions
b) Conditions, warranties and innominate terms
c) Conditions and warranties
d) Conditions, terms, and innominate terms.

ANSWERS

Formation of the Contract

1) c; 2) c; 3) c; 4) b; 5) a; 6) b; 7) c; 8) b; 9) b; 10) b; 11) d; 12) d; 13) c; 14) b

Privity, Capacity and Contractual Terms

1) b; 2) b; 3) a; 4) d; 5) b; 6) d; 7) c; 8) a

Vitiating Factors and Frustration

1) b; 2) d; 3) b; 4) b; 5) b; 6) d; 7) b; 8) c; 9) a; 10) a

Breach of Contract and Remedies

1) c; 2) c; 3) b; 4) b; 5) c; 6) a; 7) b

RECOMMENDED READING LIST

Adams, J. N. & Brownsword R., 'The Ideologies of Contract', (1987) 7 Legal Studies 205.

Atiyah, P., 'Economic Duress and the Overborne Will', (1982) 98 Law Quarterly Review 197.

Atiyah, P., *The Rise and Fall of Freedom of Contract*, OUP, 1979.

Atiyah, P., *Essays on Contract*, OUP, 1986.

Beale, H., 'Damages in Lieu of Rescission for Misrepresentation', (1995) 111 Law Quarterly Review 60.

Beatson, J. & Friedman, D. (editors), *Good Faith and Fault in Contract Law*, OUP, 1995.

Berman, H. J., 'The Law of International Commercial Transactions (Lex Mercatoria)', (1987) 2 Emory Journal of International Dispute Resolution 235.

Block-Lieb, S., 'Soft and Hard Strategies: The Role of Business in the Crafting of International Commercial Law', (2019) 40 Michigan Journal of International Law.

Bonell, M. J., *An International Restatement of Contract Law: the UNIDROIT Principles of International Commercial Contracts*, 3rd edition, Martin Nijhoff Publishers 2005.

Brownsword, R., *Contract Law: Themes for the Twenty-First Century*, 2nd edition, OUP, 2006.

Burrow, A., & Peel, E. (editors), *Contract Formation and Parties*, OUP, 2010.

Burrows, A., *Remedies for Torts and Breach of Contract*, 4th edition, OUP, 2019.

Capper, D., 'The Unconscionable Bargain in the Common Law World', (2010) 126 Law Quarterly Review 403.

Cartwright, J., *Misrepresentation*, 5th edition, Sweet & Maxwell, 2019.

Chen-Wishart, M., 'In Defence of Consideration', (2013) 13 Oxford University Commonwealth Law Journal 209.

Chen-Wishart, M., 'Undue Influence: Vindicating Relationships of Influence', (2006) 59 Current Legal Problems 231.

Christou, R., *Boilerplate: Practical Clauses*, 8th edition, Sweet & Maxwell, 2019.

DiMatteo, LA., *International Contracting: Law and Practice*, 4th edition, Wolter Kluwer Law & Business, 2016.

Endicott, T., 'Objectivity, Subjectivity and Incomplete Agreements' in J Horder (editor), *Oxford Essays in Jurisprudence*, 4th Series, OUP, 2000.

Enonchong, N., *Duress, Undue Influence and Unconscionable Bargains*, 3rd edition, Sweet & Maxwell, 2021.

Fried, C., *Contract as Promise: A Theory of Contractual Obligation*, 2nd edition, OUP, 2015.

Goode, R., 'Usage and Its Reception in Transnational Commercial Law', (1997) 46 International & Comparative Law Quarterly 2.

Gree, S., 'The Interpretation of Commercial Contracts', (2001) 117 Law Quarterly Review 358.

Hedley, S., 'Keeping Contract in its Place: Balfour v Balfour and the Enforceability of Informal Agreements', (1985) 5 Oxford Journal of Legal Studies 391.

Hill, S., 'Flogging a Dead Horse – The Postal Acceptance Rule and E-Mail', (2001) 17 Journal of Contract Law.

Hogg, M., 'Fundamental Issues for Reform of the Law of Contractual Interpretation', (2011) Edinburgh Law Review 406.

Hooley, R., 'Damages and the Misrepresentation Act 1967', (1991) 107 Law Quarterly Review 547.

Hope, D., 'The Role of the Judge in Developing Contract Law', (2011) 15 Jersey and Guernsey Law Review 6.

Klass, G., Letsas, G. & Saprai, P. (editors), *Philosophical Foundations of Contract Law*, OUP, 2014.

Lord Grabiner, 'The Iterative Process of Contractual Interpretation', (2012) 128 Law Quarterly Review 41.

Lord Hoffmann, 'The Achilleas: Custom and Practice or Foreseeability', (2010) Edinburgh Law Review 47.

Lord Nicholls, 'My Kingdom for a Horse: The Meaning of Words', (2005) 121 Law Quarterly

Review 577.
MacDonald, E., 'Incorporation of Contract Terms by a "Consistent Course of Dealing", (1988) 8 Legal Studies 48.
Macmillan, C., 'Rogues. Swindlers and Cheats: The Development of Mistake of Identity in English Contract Law', (2005) Cambridge Law Journal 711.
McGauchran, J., 'Implied Terms – the Journey of the Man on the Clapham Omnibus', (2011) Cambridge Law Journal 607.
Mckendrick, E., 'Breach of Contract and the Meaning of Loss', (1999) Current Legal Problems 53.
Mckendrick, E., 'English Contract Law: A Rich Past, an Uncertain Future', (1997) 50 Current Legal Problems 25.
Mitchell, C., & Mitchell, P. (editors), *Landmark Cases on the Law of Contract*, Hart, 2008.
Morgan, J., *Contract Law (Great Debates in Law)*, 3rd Edition, Red Globe Press, 2020.
Moss, S., 'Why the United Kingdom Has Not Ratified the CISG', (2005) 25 Journal of Law and Commerce 483.
Neyers, J., Bronough, R., and Pitel, S. GA. (editors), *Exploring Contract Law*, Hart Publishing, 2009.
Rawlings, R., 'The Battle of the Forms', (1979) 42 Modern Law Review 715.
Simpson, AWB., *A History of the Common Law of Contract: the Rise of the Action of Assumpsit*, OUP, 1987.
Smith, J. C., 'Common Law – Mistake, Frustration and Implied Terms', (1994) 110 Law Quarterly Review 400.
Smith, S., 'Contracting under Pressure: A Theory of Duress', (1997) Cambridge Law Journal 343
Smith, S., *Contract Theory*, Clarendon Press, 2004.
Stevens, R., 'The Contracts (Rights of Third Parties) Act 1999', (2004) 120 Law Quarterly Review 292.
Steyn, J., 'Contract Law: Fulfilling the Reasonable Expectations of Honest Men', (1997) 113 LRQ 433.
Tettenborn, A., 'Agreements, Common Mistake and the Purpose of Contract', (2011) 27 Journal of Contract Law 91.
Thompson, M., 'Wives, Sureties and Banks', (2002) Conveyancer and Property Lawyer 174.
Treitel, GH., 'Conditions and Conditions Precedent', (1990) 106 Law Quarterly Review 185.
Treitel, GH., *Frustration and Force Majeure*, 3rd edition, Sweet & Maxwell, 2004.
Treitel, GH., *Some Landmarks of Twentieth Century Contract Law*, OUP, 2002.
Whittaker, S., 'Unfair Contract Terms, Unfair Prices and Bank Charges', (2011) 74 Modern Law Review 106.
Willett, C., 'Re-theorising Consumer Law', (2018) 77 Cambridge Law Journal 179.

INDEX

G

H

I

J

L

M

N

O

P

Q

R

Made in the USA
Monee, IL
04 November 2026

67384330R00115